HORSES IN
THE SAND

HORSES IN THE SAND

a memoir

LORRIE POTVIN

INANNA memoir series

www.inanna.ca
Toronto, Ontario, Canada

CONTENTS

ix	*Prologue*	*Breaking Free*

Part 1   Home

3	Chapter 1	The Beginning
10	Chapter 2	Relationships
14	Chapter 3	The First Winter
21	Chapter 4	Overcoming
31	Chapter 5	The Finish

Part 2   Life's Journey

41	Chapter 6	Chain Wallets and Zippers
49	Chapter 7	Never to Be
63	Chapter 8	Brothers
78	Chapter 9	Red Seal
91	Chapter 10	Horses in the Sand
103	Chapter 11	I Know Nothing
118	Chapter 12	40 Years a Viking
133	Chapter 13	40 Years Continued
145	Chapter 14	I'm Still Counting

155	*Epilogue*	*The Road Home*
175	*Acknowledgements*	

PROLOGUE

BREAKING FREE

After I trashed the skirts I wore during my years working as a secretary, I never thought I'd wear a gown-like piece of clothing again. Once I found out from the office supervisor that nice slacks would substitute perfectly and still meet with the boss's approval, I threw them into the garbage. They were an unexplainable burden, and it didn't occur to me at the time to be disturbed about feeling like I had to present myself as feminine in order to do my job and get paid for it. I was relieved and happy because wearing a skirt felt so foreign and made me self-conscious and fearful.

Today, I'd say the reaction I had as a teenager was because the skirt identified me as female, and it was being female that made me a target, singled me out as prey.

I was seventeen when I went to the Elgin Theatre alone. It was as much to say I'd been to the Elgin as it was to see the film. A man came and sat beside me. He put his hand on my leg and began to masturbate. I sat there frozen in place, seemingly unable to move a limb or call for help, my heart beating rapidly, staring at the screen until he finished.

At a softball tournament fundraiser at an Irish bar on Rideau Street, a guy asked me to go out to his car to drink from a bottle he had in his glove compartment. He forced my head into his crotch, and I choked while he ejaculated.

In my last year of high school, I was at a party with some older boys. A hockey player dragged me into a bedroom, pulled me on top of him, and rubbed me back and forth on his erection until he groaned loudly.

My brother John told me how it got around the dressing room that this guy had "had" me. They said I was easy, a slut.

But circumstances and outlooks change as life goes on. Years later, I wore a black gown when I stepped up onto the platform to receive my diploma from the dean of the faculty of education at Queen's University.

The convocation ceremony was thrilling. I had always scorned those who went to university and got educated. They couldn't possibly know how hard it was to make a real living. How could you do real work without getting dirty, anyway?

How quickly did I change my attitude when I was accepted into their hallowed halls of higher education? Quick enough to feel foolish. Now I'm old enough to know I was jealous, feeling left behind and left out.

I'm not jealous today. Thirty years after I wasn't allowed to take shop in high school, I became a shop teacher. I graduated with basic and advanced qualifications in Transportation, giving me the credentials I needed to teach auto shop. Over the years, I went back to Queen's during the summers to get extra qualifications in Manufacturing so I could teach welding. Eventually, I also became a specialist in Special Education.

Life got a little tough for me right after university. I graduated in May 2003 and had my first major multiple sclerosis relapse that September. It began as an initial tingling in the bottom of my feet, but within five days I was numb from the hips down. An MRI showed bright spots on my spine and lesions in my brain.

Nurses from community home care came to my unfinished house in the bush to give me an IV of steroids every day for a week to reverse the attack. As soon as I was able to drive and walk without falling over, I did some supply teaching. This lasted until I was diagnosed with pneumonia, which was caused by the steroids. After pneumonia, I had to stumble through a painful uterine tract infection, also caused by the steroids. Even so, I stubbornly stayed on the supply list.

A young woman at my first gig in a Section 23 school asked me, "Are you a real teacher?" When I said that I was, she looked confused and said in a voice only teenage girls who know they're always right can muster, "Teachers don't wear jeans and black leather biker jackets, you know."

It wouldn't be the last time someone asked me this question. It usually came from girls who were unable to reconcile my look with what they thought a "girl teacher" should look like. I wore men's clothes and had my hair cut short, and a couple of my tattoos were visible when I wore short sleeves. The skin art made some kids gasp and point. "She's got tattoos. Cool!" The older boys would say, "Nice ink."

One day I came to school with my eyebrow pierced. I'd impulsively gotten it done when I was in a local tattoo shop adding to my body canvas. The students thought it was "the bomb" and "pretty sick," and I got mostly encouraging comments from the teachers I worked with. One even told me she'd thought about getting one for herself, but it wouldn't fit her look since she was on track to become a principal.

When I got my brow pierced, no one asked, "Why would you do that?" like some had with my tattoos. But I asked myself that very same question about the piercing when I almost ripped it out of my eyebrow with the headband of the welding helmet. I caught the top ball several times, and after an especially bad tug that caused a steady bleed, I took it out.

Walking down the hall in high school is very much like walking down the street or in the mall; you meet people who either like your look or don't. I was a tech teacher, and we were all considered to be a little different. This was partially because our trade licences and work experience became our undergraduate degrees. While we were allowed to take the same teachers' programs as people with degrees in Art, Music, English, or History, we didn't come pre-packaged with the lushness and knowledge—and, in some cases, the naivety—of the university experience. We came from the grind of workshops and garages and the shop floors of factories. We could be gnarly and tough, but we were also caring people committed to teaching our trade and sharing our knowledge. And sometimes it wasn't pretty, the gnarly appearing during the caring and sharing, in those teachable moments, but it worked.

During my second year, I'd been hired at a country high school south of Ottawa, and I'd been assigned a grade-eleven Construction class. On my first day, whenever I turned my back to write on the board, I was peppered with plastic pellets, the kind you'd use in air-powered rifles and BB guns. There were a few chuckles. Of course, every time I turned around, the students all had their heads down, some writing furiously as if to say, "it wasn't me." I picked a few pellets up off the floor to confirm that they were indeed real, and I wasn't dreaming. I asked the class to open their books to answer some safety questions and walked slowly around the classroom doing a slalom between workbenches. I found the culprit in the back row—what gave him away was that he couldn't stop laughing. I stopped in front of the bench he was sitting at and put out my hand. "Give it."

He looked up, grinned, and grunted, "Wasn't me."

I picked up an elastic. "This is what you've been using for your slingshot. Now give it up." I waited and then waited some more. The class went quiet as I stood there unmoving with my hand out.

He finally lifted his head. "Okay, okay. Here." He reached into his pocket, emptied it, and shoved a small handful of pellets and elastics into my hand. "There. Happy?" When I turned and walked back towards the blackboard, he asked loudly, "Hey, can I get them back after class?"

At the end of lunch on the same day, I saw him huddled with another student in front of a row of lockers. He wasn't hard to miss since he was easily the tallest kid in the school and one of the biggest. He had short blond hair and wore cowboy boots, and it seemed like he was trying to grow a moustache. Instead of turning into the tech office, I continued down the hall, stopped behind him, and tapped him on the shoulder. He turned to face me and had to lower his head because I stepped into his space like I wanted to share a secret.

I leaned in, twisted my head so I was speaking directly into his ear, and whispered harshly, "If you ever shoot pellets at me again, I'll rip your head off and shove it up your ass."

He straightened up like he'd been slapped. "Yes, miss. Sorry, miss. No problem, miss."

Carl would become my best student. He struggled with measurements and math, but he had steady attendance, did his best, helped other students, and cleaned the shop without needing to be told or asked. When he wasn't able to find someone to fund his final project, I purchased some wood and asked him to build me a small coffee table. It was a little crooked and didn't quite sit level, but its backstory made it beautiful, perfectly imperfect.

It worked out for me with Carl, but I never repeated those words or anything like them to another student. The stress of imagining myself being fired during the months that followed the locker moment was too much. Instead, I perfected the look. The stance and attitude that said, "You don't understand. I'm... going... to... fuck you over."

I didn't have to give many students the "look." This was mostly because kids really like shop. They show up early or on time, do their work, learn willingly, and take pride in the trade culture. A few don't and are just passing the time, and that's okay, but I always hoped they had a passion for something. They usually did; it just wasn't my class.

During my last assignment at a technical high school in Ottawa, teachers called me from study hall because students were asking if they could come down to my shop instead. I always said yes to the ones I knew would do the work and play well with others, good role models with initiative.

It was my last assignment because, almost eight years after my MS diagnosis, I eventually ran out of steam and had to medically retire. The toll of physically supervising and working the shop floor with twenty or more active students all day, every day, wore me down. I was exhausted.

My running out of gas at fifty could also be attributed to the early years I worked in the trades—exposure to the chemicals, gases, dust, and hazards in the shop—and the deep depression that ran me down during the years I spent teaching at Algonquin College.

College professors didn't need teaching qualifications. Our competence was evident from our trade licences and work experience. When I left my position with the city of Ottawa, my trade skills were at the highest level, and I took pride in the quality of my work. That pride was returned to me by the women and men I taught.

I didn't know anything about teaching when I was hired at Algonquin, and it showed. I stumbled my first few months, and while I gradually got more and more comfortable with being a teacher and standing up in front of others, I never got to the point where I considered myself good enough while I worked there. It felt like I was being continually judged and measured as unfit and lacking, both by the academic faculty and by some colleagues in my trade sections. It was my own internalization—I know this now—but at the time, the self-judgment manifested itself in other ways; I was overeating and drinking every day to numb and soothe myself and to stuff down my fear. In the almost twelve years I worked at the college, I went through phases where I couldn't effectively cope. I disappeared when this happened, calling in sick for weeks and months. I was hospitalized once for trying to kill myself, but most of my sick days were spent alone sitting in my basement, watching television, smoking, drinking beer, trying hard to stay invisible, and ignoring life. Give me some facial hair and a few different body parts and I'd be my brother John's clone.

There were bright spots. A few summers ago, I damaged the back bumper of my new truck and took it to the local body shop to see about repairs. A former student of mine, Troy, was running the place. We shook hands and then hugged and quickly caught each other up on the last twenty-five years.

"You know when I was working in London, the guys there always complained about women in the shop. I told them the best teacher I ever had was a woman and that she'd kick their asses any time, on any job."

I drove away that day feeling special. Spiritual leaders and mystic poets all say, in one variation or another, that to appreciate and know the goodness and the light of life, you have to experience the darker, more desperate sides of it.

I've been desperate and have tenancy in the dark side. We all walk with our own pain and burdens. In this, I know I'm not alone, and I'm grateful today for every experience I've had, for what those painful times have taught me. I'd never have learned those lessons without my trauma. While it wasn't difficult to identify my post-traumatic stress, when I look deeper on the better days, I also know I've thrived.

Many people say that they'd do their lives over exactly the same if given a second chance. If I were offered the opportunity, I'd like to do some things differently. When I was in pain, drunk, and angry, I didn't make good decisions. I hurt people close to me, and I hurt the co-workers and students I wasn't present or available for, especially at Algonquin. While I objected to a lot of the 12 Step programming, I have made amends to the people I needed to.

Ironically, it wasn't hitting a bottom that got me sober; it was the opportunity to go to Queen's for the Technological Teacher Education

Program that dried me out. When I was accepted, it was like a dream come true, a chance to learn, and an opportunity to finish my work life in a career as a teacher. I was one of twenty-eight candidates out of the almost three hundred who had applied. I felt special and valued, and I knew then that it was a once-in-a-lifetime opportunity. I didn't want to fuck it up. So, I got dry within weeks of starting school, and I've been sober since.

* * *

There are days now I wish I'd become a History or English teacher instead. I loved teaching and being with kids, and I believe I'd still be in the classroom if I taught a less physically demanding subject. I was going to add "less cerebral," but anyone who's ever had to design solutions to the innumerable problems that come up on the shop floor would know that was a disservice.

* * *

Teaching is special, and most of the teachers I worked with were there for the kids and loved being in the classroom. Unfortunately, there were teachers who should not have been teaching: the ones who got into the job because it was a career with good money and summers off, people with power and control issues, or narcissists who liked to preen and strut in front of a captive audience in the classroom.

Then there were those teachers who were predators. I stood beside one in my gown on the platform at our convocation. The classmate I stepped up with would be dismissed five years later for sexual assault and sexual exploitation of four girls under the age of sixteen. Brian Jones was sentenced to three and a half years in prison.

We were beside each other on the stage because the first two letters of our last names were the same. Brian and I also did our practicum together, and I never recognized that he was a pedophile creep. He didn't strum any weird notes, and he came across as a nice guy—he was married with kids—and a decent teacher. He was the worst type of predator, a premeditated planner. He put up a one-way shade on the window of his office so others couldn't see in, and he installed a camera in the hallway outside the door of his classroom so he could monitor the hall when he had the girls alone. Motherfucker.

When I heard about him facing charges, I remarked to a fellow teacher that the dean of education specifically told us not to have sex with our students. She told us she needed to give us that direction because some teachers, when caught, used the excuse "they didn't tell me not to have sex with my students."

Tragically, most people talking about his charges were using the news as fodder for lunchroom gossip, completely ignoring the impact of his assaults on the girls.

It was my sincerest wish that they were supported and loved. While I believed there was never any closure from being sexually assaulted and diminished, I hoped they had somehow found the space for healing and peace.

When Brian was sentenced to jail for his crimes, I was working in Brockville, teaching in an employment program for kids with behaviour issues. I miss this job the most because I had a deep connection with the students. The kids all struggled with self-esteem and self-care; most came from fragile, addictive, unhealthy, and abusive homes. They lived in a world where there was never enough of anything, especially love, tenderness, and joy. These kids were me.

My job was to teach the students skills to make them ready for employment because, for a number of circumstances beyond their control, most would not graduate high school. We would start the day by feeding whoever was hungry, and then we'd check in and plan our daily schedules.

At the bell, the older students would make their way to the classes they were comfortable attending. For the rest, we'd do some in-seat instruction for the basics in math and English. Then we would go to the welding shop or the machine shop, or play softball in the summer and basketball in the gym during the winter.

We would make time through the day to take a food inventory, talk about nutrition, make lists, and go shopping for the breakfast program. Or we would venture out to the second-hand store to find deals and look for items we could use for projects—like used cutlery for making wind chimes.

At Christmas every year, we made turkey and all the fixings for a meal, and we would invite the principal and vice-principals—or other staff that the kids wanted to share their efforts with—to come and eat with us.

I did little things for them, like keeping a bowl of fruit on my desk. All were welcome to help themselves, but they had to ask for one before taking it. It was a simple way to get the kids to ask for what they needed instead of stealing it.

"You stole a car?"

"Yeah, how else were we gonna get home?"

"You need to take off those running shoes and give them back."

"But I can't, Miss J., I threw my other ones out."

"Where'd you get the phone?"

"My uncle."

Sometimes I would accompany a student to an academic class to gauge if they could transition into more mainstream programming. Sometimes the class worked for them. But after being called "stupid" or "a fucking retard" the exercise that day became "we need to empty the classroom, wait for assistance, and be ready to call the police." The kids were a tough crowd, but once you earned their trust, they'd take care of you.

I was only ever afraid of one student who came to our program. He was really aggressive, a bully, and primal in his obsession with having things go his way. Kevin was tall and wide through the shoulders with long, lanky arms and red hair. He liked to intimidate the staff, and when I made a decision he didn't like, he'd come into my space and hover over me with his fists clenched.

He was immune to any kind of reason or compromise. I never backed away—I knew if I did it once, he'd be all over me—but I remembered the trembling and my stomach feeling sick.

One day Kevin came to school with a bandana. He wore it on his head because he wanted to be like a soldier in his war video games. Hats or head coverings weren't allowed in the school, and after I took the bandana during an assembly, he cornered me in the amphitheatre. He wouldn't let me out the main door, so I went up the stairs to go out the door on the second floor. He managed to run up and around the hall and meet me coming out the door. He ripped my keys out of my pocket using the lanyard and started taunting me with them.

I didn't know it then, but a couple of students from the program had realized what was happening and had followed him to help me out. Cody, who had run away from school a couple of times during shop class after I had re-directed his horseplay, snuck up behind him, grabbed the keys out of his hand, and gave them back to me.

As a teacher, you wanted to teach, help, and care for kids, giving them the best experiences possible while keeping your professional distance and staying safe. It was a difficult balance to strike, and the length and richness of the distance was different for every teacher.

The second year I was in Brockville, I organized what was to become an annual day trip to my house on the lake. I brought the students from the employment and developmental programs. One other teacher and a couple of educational assistants would come with us, and we'd spend the day swimming, fishing, playing, and indulging in a barbeque lunch with burgers, sausages, chips, pop, and whatever dessert we could scrounge up. It was always a great day with no behavioural issues or fights, and every year when we left, the kids would ask when they were going to come back.

The last year I taught in the program, I asked the students if they wanted to go camping at the lake instead and make it a two-day field trip. They were all in. We organized the group into meal crews to plan menus and make up shopping lists. To fundraise money for some sleeping bags, we made coat hooks and plant stands out of rebar in the welding shop and sold them to staff. It took a couple of months to get permission, plan the days and activities, gather equipment and food, and pack, but we got it done.

When I was in the staff room, I mentioned the trip, and a colleague who was an English teacher asked, "why would you ever bring them to your home?"

I looked down and mumbled, "we've been going out to my house every June, and nothing has ever happened."

In one of those do-overs I talked about wanting before, I would have told him the best times of my childhood were when I was out of the cages the adults had built for me, when I was in the bush camping, picking berries, fishing, laughing, playing, swimming, making a fire, and running free.

Those times saved my life as a child.

Similarly, as an adult, I've taken road trips to break out of those same cages, to get away, and to explore. Mostly to search out those special places, the ones beyond the bars where you can ponder life and find your true self.

I would have also told him that dreams do come true, like building a house of my own in the bush at the side of a lake.

PART 1
HOME

CHAPTER 1
THE BEGINNING

IN THE SUMMER OF 2019, I drove in the last screw holding the bottom stair rail to its post. The *rat-a-tat-tat* of the drill echoed sharply through the acreage of trees and across the mirror-like surface of the lake. It only took a few seconds for the drill to stall, satisfied with the set of the Robertson screw. The railing was done; the last screw had been screwed. I sighed heavily when I stood, the moan coming from finishing the porch stairs as much as it did from the pain of my back and knees trying to right themselves.

The day was unusually hot and humid for early June. The heat was more like what we had come to enjoy in mid-July at the peak of summer. I climbed the newly built stairs and sat with a heavy thump on the top step. Sweat stung my eyes; I pulled up my t-shirt with both hands and wiped the dirt and sawdust off my face. The last black flies of the season, a pathetically determined bunch, hovered around my face and ears. I swiped a few from my hairline, but they quickly returned, an annoying fog.

With the stairs and railings done, I'd finally completed the big porch renovation I started last summer. My happiness with finishing the project was tempered by the ache of my knees and how quickly a few hours of work drained my energy. Toiling in the heat had beaten me up. I had to alternate between working and sitting, sometimes working while sitting. It worked for me that day, but it wasn't always so.

Twenty-two years earlier, I proudly posted the building permit on the white pine that towered over the house and shed its needles on the new porch. I was young, strong, excited, and happy, filled with a dream of building a place of my own.

I'd put the stiff yellow cardboard permit I received from the township into a plastic sheath to protect it from the rain. The instructions required it to be posted in a conspicuous spot on the building site so that anyone passing by would be advised a permit had been issued for construction and could make out the inspection schedule if needed. I wasn't sure why I bothered putting it up. The lot was on a dead-end lane leading to a small private lake with no public access. There was no crowd wanting to know what was happening in their neighbourhood. Maybe I was proud?

I only had four neighbours. Except for one, all were the original property owners. We got to know each other around the fire during the early days of camping on the land. When a warm shower was a black bag strung from a tree, and the toilet was a hole in the ground that lined up with a similar one cut out of a plastic lawn chair with shortened legs. We had come to rely on and help each other through years of building outhouses, docks, decks, sheds, garages, and houses.

The plastic sheath didn't work as well as I hoped, and I took the permit down after it got soaked and stained during a couple of rainstorms. It was missing a couple of corners, the faded details nearly indiscernible. While I wanted to save what minutiae was left, I wanted the physical permit more, to be able to touch and feel it, so I crammed it in the middle of a folder labelled *House Stuff*.

The porch design accommodated the white pine that had become a steady friend for its shade. A few years before, when the porch existed on paper only, northern flying squirrels launched themselves from the tree's boughs and glided over onto the metal roof. I naïvely thought at first that the sound of them landing was pinecones falling from the tree, somehow always dropping around ten o'clock at night.

I learned quickly that when you build in the bush, the temperamental forces of Mother Earth—the wind, water, and fire, along with her plant and animal nations—immediately start taking over. Some would say they were claiming rightful ownership of their world by resisting our intrusion. Footpaths got overgrown; laneways narrowed with sumac and raspberry bushes; outhouse shingles curled back on themselves; moss and lichen grew on docks and steps; mice nested in crawlspaces and car air filters; wasps and birds built nests on any viable overhang; porcupines gnawed on siding; bears ripped metal garbage boxes from their moorings; freezing rain coated roads and driveways with ice, while flash storms washed them out; and microbursts uprooted trees and threw around canoes and dock chairs like an unhappy child would with toys in a sandbox.

Of course, I didn't know any of that when I tacked the permit to the pine. I also wasn't prepared for the many personal challenges that would come from taking on this project. Even if I had known or been warned, it wouldn't have made any difference. I was blissfully unaware and full of confidence that I would build a house.

I didn't have any savings of my own to buy the property, but I had always worked and paid my bills, so I went to the bank and managed to purchase the property using a couple of credit lines and a collateral mortgage.

I told myself that, while most of my friends made regular car payments, I would make land payments instead. Since I could fix the junker cars I bought cheap, I figured I could afford the three hundred dollars a month. I'd find out ten years later that it had become impossible to pay off the collateral mortgage because of interest and discharge fees that I didn't quite understand at the time.

Five years after buying the lot, I hired a local guy to come with his backhoe to dig for the footings and then a local bricklayer to do the concrete block for the foundation. It took four days to complete. I helped hustle and mix bags of mortar, stacked blocks, and tooled the joints between the blocks smooth when the mortar was almost dry but workable.

I was a drinker, and that first summer of construction, I borrowed a keg fridge I'd painted for a friend. I sprayed it a silver metallic, and before I clear coated it, I brushed in a rendering of the mountains from the Coors Light brand. A separate carbon dioxide tank carbonated the keg. I set the fridge up on a small platform beside a shed I had built some years earlier. The small building provided storage and, with a bunk, was a welcome alternative to several summers of tenting.

A hydro line had been installed to service all the properties along our lane, and I paid for a pole to be sunk near the back of the shed. I ran extension cords from a small breaker box installed on the pole to supply power for the building site, the shed, and the beer fridge.

The guy at the Beer Store was not initially as enthusiastic as I was about ordering in kegs. He insisted on a deposit in person. After I faithfully paid for and picked up the first keg, he gladly took phone orders. We—friends, family, and neighbours—drank our way through six kegs that first summer. The drinking and building routine was the same most days. The only rule, a simple one: we only drank after we laid down the power tools.

I remembered that first summer being gloriously sunny and warm—ideal for building. It must have rained at times, but it never impacted construction in any significant way.

My partner Sue and I invited everyone we could think of to come and help us. Family and friends came from Sudbury, Ottawa, Toronto, and places in between for a weekend or a few weekdays out of their summer holidays to help.

We built the main beam and installed the floor joists before laying the sheathing for the floor. After it was laid, we started with the walls. I'd measure, cut, and lay out the wall studs, plates, headers, and openings before the crew hammered the pieces together on the platform. I remembered teaching my friends what *flush* meant when hammering two pieces of wood together and then how to use the claw end of the hammer when things weren't so flush.

When the wall was assembled, we would square it up and sheath it using oriented strand board, or OSB, nailing the sheets firmly into place before putting out a call for the neighbours to come and help us raise it. The process of raising the first wall was orchestrated beautifully—we all counted to three, and then the crowd of souls grunted and groaned to lift it into place. After it was levelled and supported, we sat in circles drinking cold draft beer, talking tools, admiring our work, and sharing laughs while reliving some flush and not-so-flush moments.

Around sundown, there was usually a jump in the lake to wash off the day's sweat and sawdust before a barbeque dinner of burgers and hot dogs accompanied by whatever salads or sides people brought.

We had the best times around the campfire after dinner when our neighbours, Buddy and Marilyn, and their musical friends would play guitars and sing popular folk songs. Yes, "Kumbaya, My Lord" was on the playlist.

My cousin David came from Sudbury for a couple of weeks to help construct the second floor. When I picked him up at the bus station, he held a family-size box of Fruit Loops and carried a small bag. The day earlier, I got a call from my Uncle Ken asking me to make sure David didn't smoke or drink or otherwise get led astray. His family were Jehovah's Witnesses.

I laughed awkwardly when I assured Ken that his son wouldn't do any of those things—little did he know that I had already bought Davey a carton of cigarettes. I could still see him as he lay on the ground underneath the tap, his mouth open, trying to swallow the beer streaming out of the fridge.

The design for the second floor started with five-foot half walls onto which scissor trusses, so-called because they resembled the blades of open scissors, were installed to create a sloped exterior roof as well as a cathedral ceiling that reached eleven feet at its peak. The open floor plan allowed for a great room with a railing on the second floor overlooking the space below.

By the time the trusses were dropped in the driveway, summer was fading, leaving only Sue and myself at the site. With the help of Bill, a local carpenter, we were able to maneuver the trusses, one at a time, through a door, up a ladder, and onto the wall. We also hauled up all the lumber to tie the trusses together. It made for a couple of tough, long, foot-dragging days.

I spent the last of my construction money on a metal roof. With a sixty-year lifespan, it would likely never need to be changed during my lifetime. This, among others, was a very appealing incentive, but it meant I had to downsize my expectations elsewhere. I chose windows.

After some digging, I found a selection of used cedar windows that had been pulled from rows of townhouses during a condo association replacement program. Ten windows cost three hundred dollars. I picked two that were almost five feet wide by six feet high to install in the front to give the best view of the lake.

I used my 1974 Ford half-ton to pick up the windows. The cargo weighed more than half a ton, and the truck sagged and swayed coming into the lane and going up the large, long hill to the property. I was able to heave the smaller windows into place myself, but I needed help from my neighbour Bert to set the larger windows. Each weighed a couple hundred pounds. We carried them over uneven ground and lifted them several feet up into place.

From inside, the windows looked worn and over-painted. Outside, they were ragged and soft in places. They should have been replaced years before. I had been working on a plan to install them with Paula's help. We already had some experience working together, having replaced the sliding door at our house in the city. It took some creative moving, lifting, turning, and final adjusting with a small sledge and a block of wood, but we got the heavy door in its opening, squared and level.

Most importantly, our relationship was still intact after the half day of working together. I only said that because Paula and I didn't see things in the same way. I saw six, and she saw a half dozen; I asked for a "Phillips" screwdriver, and she responded, "Is that the star?" I imagined many combined shades of red and blue, and she'd picture purple.

When we built the sauna a few years ago, we sat down and created a system for working together. At nine o'clock every morning, Paula would become my apprentice, and I could tell her what to do and how to do it. During our lunch break and at the end of the day, usually around four o'clock, I couldn't tell her what to do anymore—she was off shift.

The arrangement worked well, and we had a wood-fired sauna to enjoy any time we were at the lake. We mostly patronized it during the frosty days of winter. There was nothing like coming out between rounds to roll in freshly fallen snow, gasping and howling from the shock. I should take a moment to share that it wasn't in Paula's nature to howl and gasp while doing naked snow angels, it was mine, but I knew she wanted to.

The insulation, board and batten, and roofing tin we used for the sauna were extra materials saved from building the house. I purchased the framing materials, made my own trusses, and picked up grade B eastern white cedar from a local sawmill to line the inside walls after layering them with the sturdier tinfoil used for barbequing. For a heater, I bought a used woodstove. It was longer than it was wide, which enabled me to place it in such a way that I could feed the stove externally. I built a form around its end and then poured a small cement wall to encase the stove jacket so it could safely protrude through the wooden wall.

The sauna had a small vestibule where people could sit and change. I installed two used windows and a cedar door, scooped up from the annual Westport Garage Sale Day. I custom-made the small window in the sauna proper from a cast-off piece of red cedar decking and two pieces of oven door glass I salvaged from the yard of a local scrap dealer.

The sauna worked beautifully and stayed fired up during our women's annual winter gathering. There was always lots of howling that weekend, although not necessarily all of it sauna-related. I was very proud of the small building and just as taken with the work Paula and I were able to do together.

CHAPTER 2
RELATIONSHIPS

TWO YEARS AFTER POSTING our building permit, Sue and I broke up. We separated amicably after the initial hurt, bad behaviour, and finger pointing, even using the same lawyer. Sue got the townhouse in the city, and I got the deed to the lake property. She never once suggested that it be otherwise. I loved her for understanding how important the lake was to me.

We hadn't done any work on the house during those years. After the roof was finished and the windows installed, I buttoned up the shell with doors I'd gotten on sale at the home improvement store and asked my friend Craig for help with the soffits and fascia. I'd painted his fibreglass boat, and he made the fascia and installed the soffits to return the favour. The day we put them on, his dad Roy came and helped. I made a jig out of some scrap plywood and cut the soffit pieces to length using a plywood blade installed backwards on my circular saw, and then Roy walked them over to Craig, who was on a plank supported by a couple of ladders.

* * *

Craig and Roy no longer walk this world. Craig passed a few years after I painted his boat from an aggressive form of cancer, and Roy died when his snowmobile crashed along the river. Craig's death was tragic—he was young, and he had a family. Roy's passing didn't surprise me as speed and risk-taking were part of his nature. One time, when he was coming to the lake for a visit with Frank, another sheet metal worker, he laid his motorcycle down across a turn on the township gravel road, denting and scratching his bike's fairing and tank. The repairs were simple enough but matching the hue and depth of the blue paint was a challenge. I had to call in the local paint representative to help.

* * *

Over lunch, Roy asked me twice if I had made the stairs to the top floor. He seemed bewildered that I had been able to calculate the rise and run and do the math it took to build them. How did he know I'd failed math in high school?

His questioning reminded me of my last year of high school, sitting in a classroom staring at a drawing of a tree on a chalkboard. There was a stick figure a couple of feet from the tree, and we were to use the Pythagorean theorem to figure out the distance from the stick figure to the top of the tree.

I was lost. I felt alone and stupid and afraid to ask for help. After some time spent scratching pencil on paper pretending to solve the problem, I decided who the fuck cared how far the stick figure was from the top of the tree. Not me.

On the shop floor or the building site, I taught myself what math I needed to know because I was committed to doing the job, building a home. I have used the theory of a right-angle triangle regularly since that time to check that what I build is square.

I laid out and cut the stair stringers by hand and used reclaimed boards for the treads and ¾-inch material for the risers. The lumber came through a guy who salvaged the wood from a century-old farmhouse and outbuildings south of Ottawa. I was able to get enough lumber for both floors.

It took Sue and I several weekends to find and remove the hand-forged nails, and to clean and scrape the tongues and grooves, before separating the boards into piles of the same widths. It was dirty work, and at the end of each day we were covered in decades of dirt with the odd splinter or two that needed to be tweezered.

After I got the deed in my own name, I could scrape enough cash together to wire the house. I planned it for the long weekend of May.

Family and friends were lined up to come and help, including Paula. We'd been friends for some time and had been flirting with each other for a few weeks. We both knew the wiring weekend was going to be *the* weekend. To this day, Paula remarks, "I'm so glad you were a good kisser. We might not have worked out if you weren't." We celebrated our twentieth anniversary in 2019.

My brother Mark and our cousin Shawn, both electricians, came from Sudbury. Mark brought his partner Robin and daughter Ashley, and Paula picked up my brother John and his daughter Alex on her way to the lake from Ottawa. Several other friends also came from the city to help, bringing their own friends along.

Mark laid out the wiring plan and hung the rolls of electrical wire on a broom handle that had been fastened to wall studs with some bent nails. Heather, a friend I drank and played sports with, helped me drill holes and fasten electrical boxes while Mark and Shawn pulled wire and made connections.

Late Sunday, after two days of drilling and pulling wire, the space around the electrical panel was a bird's nest of wire ends rolled into coils. Mark stripped wire, tacked it to the backing, fed it into the panel, connected the ground wires, fastened the common white wires, and powered all the circuits by connecting the hot wires to the breakers.

Mark and I struggled with healthy communication; we each preferred sarcastic digs that sometimes lead to anger. We always wanted the other to acknowledge our struggles, but neither of us could get out of our own way or step out of our own pain long enough to offer the other support.

But watching him take a jumbled mess of wires and weave them into the electrical panel in an organized, tidy combination was like watching a piece of art being created. He was an artist with his hands and tools, his movements smooth and confident. No motion was wasted—quick flicks of the wire stripper, twisting of pliers, and turns of the screwdriver. I was amazed and proud of his knowledge and skills.

There were times, standing in the kitchen of the house he helped build, that I wished the pride I felt then was all I needed to be in a good relationship with him. Unfortunately, it wasn't enough at the time, and it wouldn't be in the future. We slowly drifted apart after the electrical weekend.

He attended Eric's trial because he was subpoenaed and came for a quick visit when our mom died, but after that it would be over sixteen years before I saw him again.

CHAPTER 3
THE FIRST WINTER

LOOKING BACK, my family failures were inevitable. It was a difficult time. Six months after the wiring weekend, I was in rehab, trying to shake my drinking. I left treatment a couple of days early to testify at Eric's trial. After the trial, I was laid off from my teaching job at the college, and a few months later, Mom died.

I went back to drinking like I'd never been to rehab. It became an experience to laugh about and to poke fun at. I was stuck in primal survival mode, spending my time ruminating, getting drunk daily, wishing my life had been different.

Paula and I had rented a townhouse in Carleton Place, a bedroom community a half-hour west of Ottawa. After the trial, Paula moved back to Hull because she didn't want to commute to work, and I left to live at the lake.

I had some sick leave and unemployment insurance, but I also took a payout from the Workplace Safety and Insurance Board for an accident I had while working at the City of Ottawa. I'd injured my knee and required anterior cruciate ligament (ACL) replacement surgery. Since I hadn't made any claims for increased disability or required any further treatment for the twelve years after the accident, the board paid out the $105 I received monthly in a bulk sum.

The money helped pay for a contractor to finish the plumbing started by a couple of apprentices from the college, people I had traded work with. I was depressed and lacked confidence. Unable to even think about planning and organizing the plumbing, much less attempt to do it myself, it was easier to drink and watch someone else do it. Until the bill came. Maybe the contractor thought I couldn't count, or I was enough of a drinker that I wouldn't bother looking at the bill.

I would get embarrassed when I thought about calling him, drunk and crying, asking him about the discrepancies on the bill. I wanted to know why he would charge me for eight p-traps when he only used six, why he had invoiced me for the four-inch connectors that I had already paid for, whether he could explain why his pricing on supplies was ten percent higher than retail prices, and how it was possible to charge me for five travel days when he and his helper only came out for four.

He cut my sloppy rant short and blamed his wife for the discrepancies: "She does the billing." He was reluctant to go through the invoice one item at a time. Even in my haze, I sensed his distaste with my drunkenness, and I quickly accepted a ten percent discount when he offered it.

I called Paula after I hung up, swearing I would write a letter to the editor of the small local newspaper about the pitfalls of supporting local tradespeople who were, in my own words, "fucking crooks." I never got around to it.

The money also paid for the insulation needed to winterize the house. I asked John to come with his friend Willie to help. They lived in a boarding house near the Byward Market in downtown Ottawa. Willie was a heroin addict with long greasy black hair and a beard, both of which were streaked with grey. He didn't talk a lot, and when he did, he tended to mumble. One day, while we were eating lunch, he freaked Paula out by etching swastikas into the top of the picnic table with his pocketknife.

John assured her they were actually backward swastikas symbolizing some East Indian philosophy, an explanation Paula never believed and was never comfortable with.

John and I managed almost a week of drinking together before we started to fight. He was a convenient target who rarely fought back, and when he did, he wasn't very forceful about it; he mostly preferred to go along to get along.

The final blowout started when I went into the utility room. John was standing on a step ladder, cutting up small bits of insulation to tuck in above the black drainage pipe from the upstairs bathtub.

"What are you doing?"

"It'll help."

"Help with what?"

"Keep the pipes from freezing."

"They aren't going to freeze because they're inside the house. Besides, they're drainage pipes, not supply ones." I told him that even if it was necessary, the job could have been done using one long strip of insulation, not by wasting time cutting up small bits.

"Okay." He stepped off the ladder, picked up his beer, and took a swallow before lighting a cigarette.

When I checked in on him an hour later, he had moved the ladder under the drainpipe coming from the shower and was pushing small squares of insulation above it.

"What the fuck, John. I told you to stop."

"I just thought…"

"Seriously?" I sneered.

"Sorry." He put the pieces down on top of the scissors he'd been using.

I spat, "No, you're not."

He looked at me; his eyes were red and watery. "Really, I am, sis. I won't do it again."

"Bullshit."

"I said sorry," he insisted. His neck flushed red, making it harder to see the Chinese symbols he had inked some years earlier.

"I don't fucking care. I'm done."

He stepped down from the ladder and leaned against the dryer, folding his arms across his chest.

"Didn't you hear me? I want you gone."

"How am I going to get home?" he asked wearily.

"I don't fucking know. Walk."

"I can't walk." He pulled a beer from the cooler.

"Put it back. It's not yours."

In hindsight, I could see that I was drunk, got triggered, and lost my shit. I raged on and on until we were both defeated. At one point, I held up a chrome-legged vinyl stool, one of many I'd picked from a barn in a township south of Montreal, threatening to throw it through the sliding door if John didn't leave. He left.

It was a cold and miserable day, sometime in late October. After twenty minutes, I went to find him. I got anxious when I didn't come across him out on the road. He'd made a wrong turn at the end of our lane, and I picked him up, coming back up a hill after he'd turned around. I drove him home the next day and apologized by buying him a case of beer.

* * *

Our mom Bev had died two months earlier, in August. I had picked up John while Craig and Mark drove down from Sudbury after we got the news from Frank, Bev's boyfriend of twenty years. It was Mark who called to tell me. Paula had answered the phone, and I asked her twice to take a message—I wasn't interested in talking with him. He told her to tell me to pick up because Mom had passed away from respiratory failure in the hospital.

At the house, my brothers and I sat around an old round table, which I'd made from a top I'd picked up from a yard sale and fastened to a cast-iron stand meant for a Singer sewing machine. I felt unsure; death had never visited us this closely before. I believed my brothers felt the same. In a way, the house was just like us, a shell, empty even of its insulation, looking for more. We didn't know how to grieve, and we covered our awkwardness with alcohol. Eventually, we started telling stories about Bev, none of them that pretty.

Mom was lonely. When we talked, she always asked how the boys, my brothers, were. I'd tell her they were okay and pulled up tidbits of their lives for her to consume. They didn't call her or go visit, and we never talked about why. It went unsaid. Craig was pretty indifferent to her presence, John was poor and struggling with addiction, and Mark was angry. He held a grudge about Bev moving out west with Frank and leaving him behind without a home when he was still in high school.

* * *

I haven't cried about my mom's death yet. I distanced myself from her by seeing her as Bev, a person who hurt me, instead of a mom who loved and cared about me, doing the best she could at the time in an abusive and violent relationship.

I wanted to honour her life with a ceremony I had yet to fully imagine. It involved water, so I suspected one day I would pick up her urn and take her to the river.

* * *

After John and Willie left, I was alone installing the insulation. It was a crappy job, and to be safe, a person should wear long-sleeved shirts, gloves, and a mask. Skin contact with the strands can be itchy and uncomfortable, and most people have an aversion to the material. I didn't, and it has never bothered me to work with it, but I understood why people didn't show up in droves to help.

One neighbour remarked, "I know I should come help, but it's insulation." The insulation may have been a factor, but I also suspected they didn't want to spend time with me. I was miserable and in a dark place, and I wouldn't have wanted my company either.

Winter was coming. The work needed to be done if I wanted to stay at the lake, so I spent two weeks on ladders and scaffolding, installing batts between the wall studs and ceiling trusses. After the insulation was in, I covered the walls and ceiling by stapling on a vapour barrier and sealing its seams using an acoustic sealer and tape.

The last two things I needed to install before the winter were a wood stove and a heat line in my water supply pipe, which led from the lake. Mark had given me a used woodstove he had yanked out of his basement. Robin, his wife, didn't like the mess that accompanied a wood-fired stove, so he installed a propane heater at their place instead. I was happy to take it. Since my insurance required an inspection, I had a professional contractor cut through the roof, install the stovepipe, and make the connections to the stove.

For a base, I'd scrounged up leftover brick pavers from my friend's driveway job. I mortared them onto a cement board base with wide seams to give the impression of cobblestone. It kind of worked, if you closed your eyes and used your imagination.

For a wall shield, I built a narrow frame and covered it with fire-grade drywall. On top of the drywall, I installed rails for an air space before screwing on stainless steel panels that had been bent into a diamond quilted pattern by my friend Frank. It passed inspection.

Lastly, I ordered a heat line to help prevent my water supply line from freezing in the winter. It was a huge expense for Paula and myself to invest in at the time, almost eighteen hundred dollars, and I remember measuring three or four times just to be sure the dimensions were correct. I felt sick when I finally pushed the button on my computer to finalize the order.

It arrived in the mail exactly when the company said it would. The line came on a reel with easy-to-read instructions. I turned off the water pump at the breaker panel and sat on a plastic milk crate in the crawlspace, looking at the reel and its parts, reading and re-reading the instructions for a half hour before I felt confident enough to cut the pipe.

In the spirit of full disclosure, a few beers may have also helped.

I cut out a small section of the water pipe and fed 117 feet of the line into the opening. The end hit the pump with a few feet left. The instructions said to pull the extra line through the tee joint until it was possible to fit and tighten the compression fittings to join the two sections of pipe back together.

After I tightened the fittings, I went upstairs and flipped the breaker to turn on the water pump. I pulled a fresh beer from the fridge, ready to either celebrate a job well done or to lament any leaks. Back in the crawlspace, I sat on the milk crate and waited. It didn't leak, and I celebrated, ready for the first freeze.

* * *

We weren't very flush with cash that first winter, and I couldn't afford to buy wood. Instead, I went into the bush to pull it out myself. Before leaving the college, I purchased a four-wheeler on a payment plan and built a small trailer to tow behind it. I made the trailer sides and bottoms from lengths of tubing and sheet metal, and for the wheel assembly I shortened a trailing axel I removed from a wrecked Plymouth Reliant.

Frank, my first neighbour on the road coming in, owned 128 acres, and he gave me permission to go onto his land and take whatever wood I needed. I didn't need to make any trails because the land had been logged a couple of times, and there were lots of tracks to follow.

Once or twice a week, I sharpened my saw in the morning, filled it with mixed fuel and oil, packed it on the back of the wheeler with extra gas and oil, tools, and files, and headed to the bush. I'd cut down standing dead trees or section up dead fall if it wasn't too punky. If I had to, I disconnected the trailer, tied up the trunks, and hauled the logs out to the road where I bucked and split them. When I got tired of splitting, I loaded the wood into the trailer and made a few trips to my woodshed to unload and stack it.

I cobbled together a woodshed out of salvaged materials from an old deck and leftover tin. In its original configuration, it was basically a lean-to attached to the north side of the house. It often attracted squirrels and other critters, and I eventually moved it after something large ate through the plastic vent and gained access to my crawlspace.

It has been three years since I stopped going into the bush to get my own wood. After fifteen years of scavenging the three bush cords it took to heat the house myself, I managed to blow out both bicep tendons from using an 8 lb maul to split the wood. It was the maul I always used and was often a little sore afterwards, but that time I was unable to lift my arms above my shoulders.

It took two months of physiotherapy to get my range of movement back. I remembered being more annoyed with the time physio took from my day than from the pain in my arms and shoulders. I received the message and started buying wood from a local farmer.

CHAPTER 4
OVERCOMING

COMING OUT OF THAT FIRST WINTER at the house into the spring, I knew I was going back to school in the fall. I'd been accepted by the Technological Education Program at the Faculty of Education at Queen's. The day I applied to Queen's was one of my typical days—I got all my stuff done in the morning so I could start drinking early. It was December, cold and dark, and after dinner, I thought I should go apply. I hadn't done any research nor figured out any dates or deadlines.

When I chugged my way on dial-up to the website, I found out it was the last day to apply to the program. I had until midnight to get my online application submitted. Whether you'd call it serendipity or fate or chance or destiny, I was very grateful for the insistent voice telling me to get started.

When I left the college, part of the package the union helped me negotiate was that they would pay for my tuition, books, and related fees if I went to school. The money from WSIB was enough for gas and groceries. Paula paid the house bills—insurance, telephone, hydro, and taxes—and there were several months through the school year when I had to ask Craig and his partner Kathy for the mortgage money. They always helped me, and when it was time for Paula to buy a new car, we gave them her old one to pay back the loans.

Three weeks into school, I quit drinking. I went out with some classmates for a couple of beers, and I haven't had a drink since. Being accepted into Queen's was a gift. I'd already hit bottom, been to rehab, and then relapsed, but this was the opportunity of a lifetime, and I didn't want to screw up.

I came out of school broke but energized, happy, and focused on getting a job teaching shop in high school. I spent the summer working for a friend repurposing furniture for a geology lab at Carleton University.

By Labour Day, I hadn't landed a full-time teaching position. It wasn't that unexpected. It would have been difficult for me to take a job because I'd been experiencing numbness and strange things happening with my lower torso. It was a feeling like I had a wedgie, but when I stuck my hand down the back of my pants to check, my underwear was always right where it was supposed to be.

The numbness and tingling started in my feet mid-week. On Friday, it was almost to my knees, and by Saturday, it was up to my hips, and I couldn't walk properly. At the end of the next week, I was diagnosed with multiple sclerosis. Disease activity was confirmed by an MRI in two places, my spinal cord and my brain.

Because of our financial situation and my health setbacks, the house remained covered in house wrap, its interior walls sealed with just a vapour barrier for years. The only chores I continued with were replenishing my firewood, weed whacking the grass, and plowing and shovelling snow.

At one point, I had to replace the house wrap. It had become thin and shredded by the wind on the west side, which faced the lake. I wrestled with a nine-foot roll on the ground, pulling out the material, repositioning ladders, going up and down them with staple guns and sealing tape. It took a couple of days, and when finished, Paula remarked at the time (I thought, quite seriously) that I had installed the barrier improperly because the writing was upside down. We laughed about it.

I went through a week of daily steroid treatments to turn my mobility around. A month later, I started to supply teach in the area and was called out to schools across the region, from Napanee to Sharbot Lake to Kingston. Not fully recovered, I walked slower and occasionally leaned against a wall or column to commute from classroom to shop and back. The work was pretty steady, and it kept me going in the house for another winter.

I got a full-time teaching position for the second semester in Cloyne, an hour and fifteen minutes from the house. I commuted in my old beater truck, a Nissan pickup. I'd replaced the rusted-out box with a flatbed that had removable sides so I could have a workbench to do odd carpentry jobs in the area. The truck almost got me through the winter. Early one morning in a late spring snowstorm, one of its front wheel bearings seized on a curvy stretch of Bolingbroke Road. I walked a couple of kilometres before I got to a house with some lights on. I called my neighbour Buddy, who came and picked me up and lent me his old Chrysler for a few weeks until I could replace the Nissan.

The next school year, I received a job offer from the Upper Canada District School Board, and Paula and I moved in together after buying a house in Hull. Our hearts and home were still at the lake, but it would be years before we were in a position to continue with its construction.

* * *

In 2010, after almost eight years of teaching shop, I medically retired. I spent most of my career commuting to Brockville, either from Hull or the lake. It was a long haul every day—an hour and fifteen minutes one way from Hull and about the same travel time from the lake.

The advantage of buying another house was that after years of accelerated payments with a short amortization, we had built up enough equity to pull out fifty thousand dollars to finish the exterior and interior of the lake house. Paula was fearful about the amount but took comfort in the fact that the money spent on the building and land was equity that would always come back to us.

I hired Adam, a local carpenter looking to establish his own business in the surrounding rural community. I'd met him at Wintergreen, an off-grid educational outfit that showcases a straw bale lodge with a living roof. It was fifteen minutes away, and I volunteered there when I could manage it, doing everything from mixing mortar for their cordwood buildings to washing dishes and cleaning up after their dinner and music series.

Adam and I assembled scaffolding to strap, insulate, and install board and batten siding. He went up and down the scaffolding and did all the heavy lifting, and my job was to cut and supply the materials from the ground. It worked well, and when we were done, the house was finally at its required R20 insulation for the walls.

We installed two dormers on the west, or lake-facing, side of the house. I originally thought to put in skylights, but I decided I didn't want to cut through my roof with skylights that didn't offer a view. I went with shed dormers instead, which would let me install windows facing the lake. It was a much bigger job than installing skylights.

To start, I pulled out the ceiling insulation I'd stuffed into the same bays years earlier and was gifted with a small landslide of dried-out rodent feces—compliments of those flying squirrels. I was very happy not to find small skeletons curled up in some nesting material. I worried I would trap them in the building while evicting them. I made an aluminum box out of a length of screening material (generally used to prevent leaves accumulating in eavestrough), added a one-way door flap in the middle and an exit cone narrowing down any attempt at re-entrance, and installed it right at the peak where they had found a way into the roof. I left it there for a week. They could leave but couldn't get back in. After a few nights of ferociously bombarding the roof, seeking a way in, they moved on.

We were reinforcing the roof trusses for the dormers when the old aluminum step ladder I used for years collapsed with me on the top step. Going down, I grabbed for the closest truss but, with my weight plus the tools I was carrying, I didn't have a chance. I landed hard on my hip and back and limped in an upright crouch for almost a week afterwards.

Adam then reached out to a friend from Kingston to help him install the ceiling. I purchased over a thousand square feet of tongue and groove pine for the installation from a local lumber yard. I set up two sets of sawhorses to support the lengths of lumber, and Marilyn came over from next door for a couple of days to help me paint the boards.

I wanted a pickling type of finish that would show the wood grain, but the cost of the solution was prohibitive. Instead, I reduced white latex paint with water until I got the finish I wanted. The ceiling was more white than pickle, and brush marks were visible, but the overall look of the ceiling fit the space.

A local drywaller who had done work for both Bert and Buddy came and gave me a quote to finish the drywall. It was reasonable, and within two weeks, both his boys were installing the wallboard.

I had already done the drywall in the downstairs bedroom and laid in a partial ceiling and walls in the adjacent bathroom so I could install the shower, sink, and toilet. Drywall was cheap and fairly easy to install, but not everyone has the patience for it, especially when it comes to mudding and finish sanding the seams. It takes practice and skill, both of which were nurtured during my work in the autobody trade.

Working alone, I lifted the sheets to the ceiling in the bedroom. I managed to balance a full sheet, measuring four feet by eight feet, on my head while I climbed the step ladder. At about fifty pounds, it was awkward to balance and position, but I was able to hold it in place with my head and shoulder while fastening it to the ceiling joists with a driver in my other hand.

While the drywall installation was successful, I was disappointed that the boys had left seams behind the railing posts on the second-floor loft. I wasn't sure why they didn't slide the sheets behind the posts—I left them enough room to do so. I made an assumption at the time and never checked in with them about it until it was too late. There were other irritants like sloppy mud work and improperly placed joints around windows, but I was very happy to not have to do it myself. I didn't complain.

The railing was a special project. Beetles had ravaged several stands of white pines around the lake and through our adjoining properties. Working on the house during the summer, when the beetles were especially active, I would stop, go quiet, and when the wind settled the rustling of the leaves, I could hear them chewing.

One winter, I cut and pulled out several dead trees, skidding them with my wheeler to a clearing beside the lane. In the spring, I borrowed a portable sawmill from Paula's dad and cut the trees into posts and boards.

I notched and lapped the beetled posts over the exposed second-floor beams and floorboards, and then I infilled each bay with horizontal boards and vertical stiles. I regretted I didn't plane the wood before installing it. I thought I'd get away with the rough finish; it worked, but it made cleaning the railings a real chore. They had to be vacuumed because wiping them was impossible.

* * *

I've left all of the wood in the house either rough or unfinished. Having spent years in an industry where I was exposed to chemicals in innumerable solvents and materials, I didn't want any in my home. However, paint technology has changed dramatically over a short period of time. There are now several green options to choose from to stain and finish wood without risking exposure to the grim compounds of older refinishing systems. There may come a time when I have the energy to remove the railings, fix the seam behind the posts, plane and finish the pieces, and reassemble it. If I am honest, that project is unlikely to ever land on my to-do list.

* * *

With the drywall finished, I installed the trim for the windows, baseboards, and ceiling. Priming and painting the interior took a couple of weeks. I worked my way from the second floor down the stairwell to the first floor. The peaked ceilings created some challenges, but the biggest obstacle was painting the stairwell. It peaked at eleven feet above the second floor. The ceiling sloped downwards as the stairs descended, but it was still fourteen feet high at the bottom of the stairs.

I built a custom step that I attached over two stairs to create a flat landing for my ladder. I could move it up and down as needed. At the bottom, I set up some narrow scaffolding with a platform and built a ramp from the stairs to meet it.

It took much more time preparing for painting and cleaning up afterwards than it did to actually do the task itself. I learned that with most successful jobs, regardless of what they are, prep work is essential if you want to get it right and be safe.

Fatigue is also a factor, and I've learned to be mindful of it, but there have been days when I've been like a dog with a bone, pushing myself to do just one more job, to finish that one last thing that needs doing. I'd "get 'er done," my stubbornness pushing my body beyond limits, then I'd relapse into a state of tingling exhaustion that took days to recover from. It was always in my nature to move and create because doing otherwise didn't feel right, but it came with a cost.

I found it difficult to practice self-care, finding that balance between work and rest. I was constantly nose-to-nose with my limitations, challenging them, even more so when I was experiencing the effects of aging and the fatigue of MS. I was afraid to stop moving because I could get to a dismal state in a hurry. Sometimes I asked myself if I was depressed because I was tired, or was I tired because I was depressed? Was I was a sad chicken or a sad egg?

* * *

The last three big projects in the budget were to finish the upstairs bathroom, tile the floor in the kitchen through to the foyer and entrance, and face the big end wall in the great room with pine.

There were the days, years even, when there were no toilets in the house, and we had to trek to the outhouse in the middle of the night. Paula would often wake me to accompany her, so it was an undeniable pleasure when I installed a toilet upstairs.

The upstairs bathroom is an extension of the bedroom. It has a free-standing tub, a toilet, a vanity, and a large glass shower. Paula picked out the tile for the floor and shower walls. Before tiling, I put in the base for the shower and ran the plumbing for the free-standing faucet.

We purchased the tub from a couple who had bought it for bathroom renovations that were never realized. It was still in plastic wrap when I picked it up with my trailer. When I got it home, I asked Buddy's daughter Alley and her partner to come over and help me hike it up the stairs.

Grouting the tile in the upstairs bathroom took my legs out from under me. I mixed grout and cleaned the pails outside using a garden hose because I didn't want any of the mix going down the drain into the septic. That meant walking up and down the stairs, in and out of the house, dozens of times. At the end of the day, it was all I could do to take my clothes off to get into the shower, my legs screaming with the effort. I fell asleep as soon as I got into bed. After a few hours, I woke up with cramps strangling my calves and thighs. Their grip was so tight I thought I'd never be able to move my legs again. The pain was extreme, and I was scared. I managed to roll out of bed and get upright. I staggered, taking small steps while beating my legs with closed fists. The beating would work on one thigh, but the cramps would return while I hit the other. The contractions were unrelenting, and it was exhausting.

It was about a week before I felt confident enough in my legs to risk carrying the shower stall sections up the stairs. The shower box was heavy; I could barely hold up my end when an employee from the building store helped me put it on my trailer.

When I got home, I slid the box out onto some boards and raised it upright in the driveway. I was able to pull it over some scrap pieces of plywood to the bottom of the stairs, where I leaned it over the stairs, through the door and pushed it up into the house like a giant domino.

There were three glass components weighing sixty to seventy pounds each. My hands were sweating with the idea of one of them breaking and having glass rain down on me and the stairs. I lifted them up, one step at a time, starting with the lightest to boost my confidence and finishing with the heaviest.

I drilled the tile wall to install the vertical pieces and assembled the rest of the shower panels in an upright position as per the instructions. I used some soft rope to secure the large pieces of glass to the railing while I worked. The next day I called Frank to come over and help me move the assembled shower stall into position. It took some shuffling and sliding, but we managed to get it up and onto the base without any damage.

The tile I chose for downstairs matched the brown in the tile Paula had picked for upstairs. I calculated the square footage and purchased it on sale from the home improvement store.

The layout took a day. The tiles I laid in the kitchen would affect the layout of the tiles in the bathroom. I wanted the tiles to be centred in each room and to have the partial tiles at the edges close to the same width—no slivers or wedge-shaped pieces. It was difficult and frustrating, but the time spent was worth the effort because I had no anxiety starting the job.

I installed a straight edge on my marks and laid the first set of tiles along it, going from the kitchen into the entrance foyer. Every tile from there on would be laid using that first set as a guide. I tackled the kitchen first, cutting tiles as I went. Where it might have taken a professional with a helper a day to do the job, it took me most of a week. My pace was slow and steady, and I made sure to keep my legs under me. I was afraid of a reoccurrence of the night cramps.

Despite my hopes, leg cramping had become more frequent, day and night, no matter how active I had been. I was thankful none had been as painful as "grout night." The intensity and powerlessness of that attack stayed with me. Since that night, I have been careful to stay hydrated and, when the cramps twisted beyond tolerance, I used medication prescribed by my neurologist to settle the pain.

I used oak for the floor transition strips between the tile and the wood. Sharon, a long-time friend who lived on Wolfe Lake, offered me a bed frame with oak rails and hardwood strips belted together to support the mattress. I ripped the rails into four strips, then planed and bevelled two edges using an adjustable bench sander. The natural colour was light, so I stained them with a water-based dark mahogany finish to match the tiles. They worked beautifully.

It was time for the big wall. I remembered sitting in my chair looking at it; it was twenty-four feet wide and fourteen feet high at its full width, peaking to six feet at its centre. It was daunting, and my legs and spirit felt fatigued just thinking about the work it would take to install the load of red pine floorboards waiting outside.

I'd ordered the pine from a local sawyer up the road. The boards were sixteen feet long, but my trailer could only accommodate ten feet. This wouldn't have been a problem if I could have removed the rear gate and let the lumber overhang the back of the trailer. But the hinge pins the gate pivoted on were pointing towards each other, making it impossible to slide it off.

I used an angle grinder to cut the welds holding the pins so that I could pick up the lumber. I later welded the pins back on using a MIG welder at my father-in-law's shop. I oriented the pins so they faced the same direction. This way, the gate could be removed and replaced as needed without cutting off the pins.

I calculated it would take thirty rows to cover the height of the wall and managed to convince myself that I just needed to do six rows of boards a day, and I'd be finished by the end of the week.

I had set up my mitre saw so that all I needed to do was to pull the boards one at a time from the trailer onto my saw support stand, cut them, and pass them through the terrace door. I stacked them on the dining room floor, ready to be installed.

The lower sections went quickly, but things slowed down once I got to the upper sections and needed to use scaffolding and ladders. The most difficult part was installing the sixteen-foot lengths of board.

From a ladder, I installed a support made from some scraps to help guide the ends of the boards into place. I then hiked up the scaffolding and wrestled the board up. Holding one end, I tried to land the other end into the guide. The boards would waver, barely catch, and then fall. After a couple of attempts, I lost strength in my arms and shoulders and had to let the board down. I rested, lifted the board, and started again, feeling like I was ring tossing at the local fair. I couldn't ever remember getting a ring over the bottles, but I do remember being determined that, given enough time and rings, I would be successful and get the prize.

It took a week. I believe this was when I tore up the cartilage in my knee—likely from the steady up and down climbing of ladders and scaffolding.

On the weekend, I asked Frank to come and help me install the vertical boards across the peak. Each board needed an angle cut, and having someone cut and hand up the boards would save me time and lessen the strain on my knee.

From the scaffolding, I measured the lengths needed. Frank would cut them at the saw and his girlfriend, Katie, handed them up. Frank was a generous, mostly happy guy, and even though he had done a lot of renovating, he couldn't seem to grasp the cuts I needed, so half of the boards handed up were wrong.

He started to get upset, and when I looked at the growing scrap pile beside the mitre saw, I began to wonder if I'd have enough material to finish the peak. I considered telling him I was tired and needed to rest, and that they could go home. Instead, I climbed down, picked a board from the pile, and walked him through the cut, showing which face needed to be up and where to measure from. I worked up a sample for him to use as a guide.

As soon as the angle of the cut switched past the centre, Frank miraculously figured it out. I supposed all he needed was a different perspective. We used most of the material from the scrap pile, and I was relieved I wouldn't have to order more wood. We even had time to install the trim board from the wall to the ceiling. It was a good day.

CHAPTER 5
THE FINISH

THE IDEA OF BUILDING a wraparound porch at the age of fifty-eight was overwhelming. When I was anxious about starting a job, I usually told myself things like *just get started, work away at the list, in a few weeks you'll be done*, and *just do it*. The mantras weren't helping this time. Paula and I talked and agreed to hire a contractor even though it would likely mean double the budget of fifteen thousand dollars.

One local carpenter, Bill, was booked ahead for a year. Another didn't return my phone calls. Yet another didn't come see the project until I had harassed him about it for a couple of weeks. Harassed is probably too strong a word. I'd left him several messages, not realizing he was out of town on vacation. When he came, he brought a friend who was interested in doing the job because he couldn't take it on at the time.

The friend seemed keen, and his buddy said he did good work. He accepted the job on the condition that I pay for his fuel costs because he'd have to drive almost an hour to get to our place. We shook hands on the deal. I was nervous about the money but looking forward to having a new porch built.

Early the next morning, he called and cancelled, saying, "If I wanted a job that big, I'd have stayed at work." I felt betrayed. After hanging up and venting a bit, I became less disappointed and more motivated. I went to work the next day.

Bert came with his tractor and backhoe attachment. I widened a path, cutting back some saplings beside the house so he could safely get around the septic and some large rocks. Bert navigated his tractor to the front of the house and started digging the holes for the builder tubes. The tubes would sit on a gravel base and be filled with concrete reinforced with rebar.

It took most of a day to dig the holes. I picked up tubes, cement, and rebar from the local building store, and aware of my limitations and wanting to get the porch done before the end of the summer, I put an ad on Kijiji seeking help with the project.

One of the first people to respond was a man who'd recently retired and moved to Kingston with his wife. I offered to send him directions twice by phone, and he kept assuring me he knew where he was going. On the morning he was coming out to look at the job, he called me twice, lost. I didn't completely understand him because of the poor service. I drove out to a popular intersection to wait for him. It was a miracle we found each other.

Vince was a small man driving a big Cadillac. When we first talked, he said, "if I stay at home, then I have to work on the wife's list. This way, I can get out of the house and make a little money." He seemed eager to do the job, especially since it was located in such "nice country." He told me he'd mixed cement before and that the job would be no problem.

We shook hands on an hourly rate of twenty dollars cash, plus some weekly gas money—the amount to be determined later. Before leaving, he offered to help me get the bags of cement off my trailer because I had to go pick up a cement mixer. I positioned a pallet beside the trailer to lay the bags on so they'd be off the ground. At sixty-six pounds each, the bags were heavy and awkward. I deadlifted one and then another, setting them in place, and then I watched him struggle to get one up off the pile so he could carry it off the trailer. He managed to get into a rhythm, wrestling one bag for my two.

Vince called me at five-thirty the next morning. When I saw his number, I let it go to voicemail. "I won't be able to get out today," he said. "My car broke down, and the wife needs the truck. I'll call you when I get it fixed." He never called.

Later that morning, I dragged and wheeled the cement mixer over to the first hole. I had filled the bottom of the hole with coarse, clear limestone to provide drainage. I levelled and reinforced a tube that I had previously fitted with a flared base for better stability. Then I sunk three lengths of rebar in a triangular set to reinforce the pour and tube stability.

The most difficult task was lifting the bags into the maw of the mixer because the opening was above my waist. The mixer held just over two bags, and it took almost five bags of concrete to fill the first tube. After pouring a second tube, my shoulders burned, and my legs shook with fatigue. I was done for the day.

I talked with my sister about the cement work I was doing. She was taken aback. She had worked as a personal support worker with people who were elderly. "You shouldn't be doing that. You could rupture your abdomen, and your guts will fall out." I got a quick visual of entrails protruding from orifices, an image I didn't need and replied, "What can I do? It needs to be done, and who else is going to do it?"

I kept the Kijiji ad up, and I heard from another man who was interested in helping. He asked lots of questions about the type of work, how much I was paying, and how far a drive it was from Kingston. I told him all I was looking for was someone with strong legs and a strong back to do the physical work I couldn't do. He responded, saying that he was strong in a lot of places and was also good-looking if I was interested in travelling down that path.

I nearly choked when I read his response. Paula laughed when I told her, saying, "Well, what did you expect when you put it out there that you needed a strong back and legs?"

"Call me naïve, but not that."

Then there was a young man named Gregory. He lived nearby with a woman who was trying to establish a spiritual healing retreat after they moved to the area from Toronto. He asked me if he was going to be supervising the job. He said he could start immediately.

Gregory was forty-five minutes late the first day. "I couldn't find any place to get coffee, so I had to drive into Verona," he said. He was tall and fit looking, in his mid-twenties, and he wore his dark hair in a man bun.

"Okay. How about if I have coffee ready for you in the mornings? Will that help?"

"That'd be awesome." He smiled.

He asked me for twenty-five dollars an hour, which was more in line with his current needs, and he promised he'd work hard for it and be on time. He seemed eager and motivated, and he was even wearing a pair of steel toe work boots. I accepted with the condition that the wage included his gas for travelling. I showed him how to move the mixer, stabilize it, and level it above the tube in the hole, and I explained what consistency the mixed cement should be.

The first batch got away from him; he wasn't prepared for how heavy the cement was and how quickly it poured out of the mixer. He knocked the tube out of alignment. After we got it repositioned, he was more careful, and the first day went pretty well. After each tube was filled, every hole needed to be backfilled carefully to keep the tube true and level. He worked mindfully with direction, and I felt confident we'd have a good relationship.

At break and over lunch, Gregory was eager to tell me about his work on the more ephemeral planes of the universe. He told me how the aligning of the astrological elements according to our own births and re-births was used to guide and heal our lives. I wasn't quite sure I understood it all, especially when he said he did a lot of his work at night, making it difficult for him to be on time in the morning. He was also on his phone quite a bit; I learned later that he was counselling someone. In which universe I didn't know.

Gregory was on time the next day. I had coffee ready for him, an expensive organic blend I picked up at the local farm store. He was pleased. When he left the previous day, he had asked me my age and birth date, and it was obvious this morning that he wanted to share his interpretations with me. I held him off until we took a mid-morning break. He was excited and animated, more so than when he was working with the cement or the stones, as he called the gravel.

I tried to pay attention when he talked about moons rising, something falling, phases, shifts, and entrances, but my mind kept going back to the load of wood that had just been dropped off by a driver from the local hardware store.

Gregory reminded me of people who have to get close physically to the person they are talking with. I suppressed the urge to move away and nodded thoughtfully, I hoped at the right times. He seemed satisfied.

The next morning, he was over an hour late. After he parked the car he was borrowing from his spiritual mentor, he came bouncing down the driveway with his guitar in one hand and what I assumed was lunch in the other. He wanted to sing me a song. I washed my face with my hands and mumbled, "what the fuck?" into the ground and suggested he get a coffee so we could talk.

"We've talked about this," I said. "I need you to be on time."

"I know, but this isn't what I do."

I could feel my face getting red and my heart knocking in my ears. "Okay." I drew the word out slowly before telling him, "I get it, but I have a budget and a timeframe." My inner voice was yelling *and I'm paying you!*

"I understand."

"I'm trying to be mindful. I don't want to be pissed and start my day unhappy. It's not fair to either of us, but I have a job to do."

Gregory looked down and started scuffing a dirt pile with his boot. "I appreciate that you are aware of different levels of consciousness."

I wasn't at all convinced that Gregory understood my position, and I went back to filling holes, consciously punching the shovel into a pile of dirt.

At lunch, Gregory pulled out his guitar and sang me songs while I awkwardly sat in a chair at the dining room table. I had covered the chair with old towels so it wouldn't get dirty from my soiled work clothes. At one point, I looked over. His eyes were closed, and his brows were furrowed, in what state I wasn't sure, and he'd let his hair down. It flowed in long waves past his shoulders. He reminded me of the cover of a romance novel.

He told me the first song was paying homage to the nations and generations of women weavers around the world and the other, a lengthy ballad with words and vocals I didn't understand, was about the water.

I bit my lip and told myself not to smile for fear it might have led to laughter. "Thanks. They were lovely. Singing about and praying for the water is important work."

The next morning Gregory was late again. He was supposed to be finishing the cement work. I decided that it would be his last day. When he arrived, he could tell I was unhappy, so he put his head down and got right to work. No preamble about moons, signs, consciousness, or, thankfully, any sight of a guitar. I relented in my death stare and told him I had coffee on if he'd like a mug.

At lunch, he asked if he could move in with me. "I'll be better with the wood than with the stones," he said.

I stood there holding a shovel, silent. *What did he just say?*

"We can carpool for groceries, and I can help with other stuff or take care of the dogs."

I nodded, keeping a neutral expression. *Whaaaaat.*

"I'd need a month's pay in advance—four thousand dollars. I'd work hard once we get to the carpentry."

Is he serious? He's serious.

"Let me talk with Paula, and I'll let you know tomorrow."

Paula was as shocked as I was. Her response was something along the lines of "fuck no."

When he rolled in the next morning, late as usual, I said, "Sorry, Gregory, but we aren't going to be able to help you out. Coffee is on."

He shrugged. "Okay, thanks for thinking about it. I have some friends in Ottawa I can move in with."

Once the cement work was finished, I walked him over to a load of clear crushed stone I'd been using as drainage for the holes. I needed most of it spread out in the crawlspace. I'd cut out the vent hole and made a chute out of two plastic pails, the ends of which had been cut out and then sliced in half. The four halves were screwed together and supported by a saddle made with some scraps of lumber.

I showed him how to shovel the gravel into the chute, pushing it down if necessary, into a waiting wheelbarrow. We went into the crawlspace, and I wheeled the material to the far corner and dumped it. I spread it with a steel rake.

"This is a flat rate job. What I'd like for you to do—if you want, because it's all I got for you right now—is to shovel for an hour and then let me know how many hours it will take for you to do the job."

Gregory shovelled for an hour. "I think it'll take two days to get the stones spread in the basement."

"To be clear, this is not a skilled job. I can't pay you twenty-five dollars an hour to shovel gravel, but I'll pay you twenty dollars for fourteen hours plus sixty dollars for gas, for a total of two hundred and forty dollars to move the pile. The whole pile. And, this is important, since it is a flat rate job, you only get paid when you finish it. You can take your time, come and go, or you can hustle and get it done in a day or two. It's up to you."

"I really appreciate your flexibility and willingness to work with me."

"I need to make it clear—no payment until it's done. I don't want to be left looking at a pile of stone I have to shovel."

A couple of days later, on a Thursday, Gregory was dropped off with some camping gear and a pack of scrounged food. I offered him a tarp for his tent, an air mattress to sleep on, and a pillow. After he set up, he'd disappear into the bush, come up and shovel for a half-hour, sit down at the dock, come up and shovel enough to fill the wheelbarrow, and then go back to the lake and sing and play the guitar.

"You know those ripples that radiate out from the dock?"

"Yes."

"I just rode one of them for twenty minutes. It was amazing."

I had to look away.

He disappeared for almost two weeks around the summer solstice before re-appearing in late June. "I had lots of energy work with shifting circumstances and alignments," he told me.

He moved gravel half-heartedly for a couple of hours before saying, "I have to leave now. Do you think you could pay me for the work I've done on the stone? It's about half done."

A generous estimate would settle on less than a quarter done. I hardened. "No. I'm sorry, Gregory. I don't have any cash on me, and besides, we had a deal. You get paid in full when the pile is done."

His smile dropped. "I understand. I'll try and get back tomorrow to finish it if I can get a ride."

That was the last time I saw Gregory. Later, I was reminded of him at times when I stepped on the dock, and the water rippled out towards the far shore. I watched the small swells and wondered if they would ever get to where they were going. Would he?

Fortunately, shortly after Gregory left, I ran into a young carpenter friend, Jared, working a coffee stand at a local farmers' market. I asked him if he needed some work, and after agreeing to a wage and some daily gas money, he followed through on his commitment to show up and be on time.

After the first day, he asked me for an advance to fix his car. I gave him what he asked for with the belief that if he didn't follow through, it still felt like it was the right decision as he was supporting a family of six. Jared didn't disappoint, and we worked hard together to finish the first stage of the wraparound porch. He was a blessing.

Bert and Buddy came over one day, and after setting up a system, we shovelled and spread all the limestone fill I needed for the crawlspace. It felt really good to see the pile diminish and land where it was intended.

Jared showed up again early in the second summer of porch construction, taking some time among his other commitments to help with enclosing the mudroom and finishing the screened-in section of the porch.

* * *

I was truly privileged to live on a small slice of the Canadian Shield, among the granite, evergreens, maples, and oaks. Where wind and rain nourished and cleansed the earth. A land where deer and wild turkeys and bears came to feed.

My days and nights filled with songs of loons and whippoorwills, hoots of owls, jeers of blue jays and squawks of crows and ravens. All I needed to do now was listen to know that dreams come true.

The hope of building a home of my own started out as a small seed, cautiously planted when I was a young girl. I wanted a home of my own that was safe, one that would envelop and protect me. That dream saved my life then, as it does now.

PART 2
LIFE'S JOURNEY

CHAPTER 6
CHAIN WALLETS AND ZIPPERS

EARLY IN THE FALL, I left Edmonton with the vague idea of travelling west to Jasper, south through the Rockies, and then hanging a left towards Calgary somewhere around Banff.

I got distracted leaving Canmore and made a right before getting a sniff of the Calgary suburbs. Then I got led astray again when I saw a sign that read *Crowsnest Pass turn right*. Curious, I turned right.

It was near nine o'clock when I missed the turn for the Crowsnest Pass tourist information parking lot. I spent the night in a pullover huddled up to a B-train whose lights I managed to see when I crested a hill in the rain.

The next morning the B-train was gone, and I silently thanked the driver for keeping his truck's running lights on while he was parked. It was very rare that I got scared when driving, but that night I was frightened. The slow, dark hill climbs descending into the black maws of the valleys became almost indistinguishable with the heavy pounding of the rain. Hypnotized by my primal survival instinct and blinded by oncoming traffic, it was nearly impossible for me to see the road, much less the division lines. Even with my wipers on full, whacking their displeasure side to side, I couldn't make anything out. The narrow, tight shoulders and lack of markers made driving the pass in poor weather an exercise in hope as much as in skill and courage.

When I crested a rise, I saw strings of lights illuminating the truck's features like a beautiful beacon of safety. I braked hard and turned right into the pullover, chewing up gravel, before slowing down enough to not hit the rhubarb and crawled around the far side of the rig. The relief was sobering. The memory of white-knuckling the steering wheel was a reminder to slow down, to stop chasing the tail of a dragon I could never catch.

From British Columbia, I dropped down into Montana at the west side of Glacier National Park. I planned to drive parallel to the parallel on my way home, travelling east through the United States. But my plans changed when I happened to purchase a map, a real paper one, and laid it out on a picnic table after turning away from the park entrance.

I left the park, not because I didn't have the right change, or the bosses didn't want a tattooed lesbian visiting because it wasn't queer day or pride week. I turned around because the ranger, wearing a real Smokey the Bear hat, suggested it wasn't a good day to visit. She explained cloud cover and told me that I wouldn't be able to see the tops of the mountains or the glaciers, and besides, it was wet and raining. She spoke with a tone and expression that implied I should've known better than to visit the park.

And she was right, I should have known better. I was relieved and quite happy to turn around. I was already looking for a way to back out politely when I learned it would cost thirty dollars in American currency to get through the gate, which is almost forty dollars in Canadian money. *Sorry, I have to take this call. Okay, okay, got it, I'll be home soon. Sorry, I have to go. My mom's sick.*

"Thanks, anyway," I said. "Nice hat."

I texted Paula: *Safe and in Montana.*

Whaaaaat? she responded.

On tour, not sure where I'm landing. All good.

Be careful.

I lingered on her response, happy that we were at least now texting. I closed my eyes and pictured how she looked one of the last times we talked in person: off work, spending hours in her chair staring at the television, struggling, sad.

I tapped out, *You okay?*

I'm good. She got back quickly.

I tucked my phone away and got back to looking at the places I'd stopped at on the map. I felt like a kid playing the leapfrog game; the world was mine, and I could go anywhere I wanted. I hoped that planning my route would prevent a reoccurrence of the previous night's run. Chasing the dragon through Crowsnest Pass was foolishness and a good way to end up dead in a ditch.

Encouraged by my change of metaphors, I ran my finger along a road. I just have to leap from this destination to that, then to this one, and over to that one, or maybe that other one. And, when I'm finished playing, I'll worry about getting home. Besides, I rationalized, all roads lead to home and back to Paula eventually.

Folding up the map, I decided to travel to Yellowstone National Park. It didn't look that far, considering the four thousand kilometres I had already travelled from Eastern Ontario. It was but one small leap.

* * *

My mother Bev called me a butch when I was in my mid-teens. She didn't mean it as a compliment. It was in the '70s, a time when disco, bell-bottom jeans, shag carpets, muscle cars, and avocado-coloured appliances were celebrated. How did she know I coveted my brother's chain wallet, the type popularized by bikers riding Harleys?

I always knew I was different from the other kids in the small town I grew up in. In grade school, girls were supposed to play with dolls, wear dresses, and pretend-hate the opposite sex. All I wanted to do was play hockey and steal crabapples with the boys. I was called a tomboy. They said it was just a phase that normal girls went through. But my time as a tomboy never ended. Bev called me out one morning after I refused to wear a dress for a co-op work placement. Her frustration that day came from years of my rejecting her when she persistently pushed me to wear dresses and use lipstick, blush, and hair products. Instead, I embraced running shoes, jeans, and at times my brother's sloppy and often dirty t-shirts. But I never stole his wallet to wear because I intuitively knew it would be unsafe. It would make me a target.

It hurt that it was my mother taking aim—a lot. I didn't quite know what the word *butch* meant at the time. I only knew that it was a putdown to describe a girl as tough and mannish looking. I was confused and ashamed, wondering what I had done wrong.

It wasn't as if I hadn't heard the word before she flung it at me—name-calling was common in our high school. We easily used insults like *chinks* to describe the boat people who came to our small town from Vietnam or *Jew* for anyone who was cheap with their money. Even the classic rhyme, *Eenie, Meenie, Miny, Moe*, wasn't spared. Parents never punished us for using those slurs or others like *spic*, *pig*, *faggot*, or *lezzie*.

One day, a rumour went around school that lezzies actually used a secret finger tickle of the palm to identify themselves to each other. We practised the tickle on each other in the school parking lot during lunch break with lots of nervous laughter and chatter. No one ever came out as a lesbian. I remember feeling simultaneously relieved and disappointed.

I must confess that I did have a lezzie moment of my own with a friend, spending a sweaty hour with her necking in the backyard treehouse at her parents' home. We were pretending to be married—pressing our bodies together and giving each other the tongue. I wasn't quite as enthused as she was. Though the idea of kissing someone while in a manly position appealed to me, I couldn't slip my tongue around her metal braces without wanting to gag. It felt like licking wet zippers, similar to the steel ones found on the bulky snowsuits we wore when sledding down Dump Hill as children. The interlude also wasn't as I imagined it should be, smooth and cool, sexy and hot. Ideas implanted by reading the numerous romance novels cast off by Bev. After flip-flopping around like some half-alive fish, alternating between being the macho top and the femme bottom, I gave up and lied about needing to get home.

Home was where I lived with three brothers. I was jealous of them, and not just because they got to wear boots and jean jackets and have chains draping from wallets stuffed into the back pockets of their jeans. I was resentful because they could take shop in school where they worked on cars and made stuff out of wood, while I was forced to sit and learn sewing, cooking, typing, and shorthand. My young confidence was squeezed out of me from being forced into those feminine roles. I could never relate and always felt out of place and inadequate. I felt like a failure. Worse, I was lonely. In order to belong, I buried the tomboy and pretended to like boys, becoming angry and resentful in the process, smothered by the feeling of being somehow not enough. The faking and denial fuelled self-hatred, and eventually,

I internalized my own homophobia. Externally, I started drinking and smoking and partying whenever I could.

At seventeen, I left home for Ottawa and got a job as a secretary. I was grateful for the paycheque, but it meant that I had to wear girl clothes while sitting at a desk typing, filing carbon copies, and answering the phones. I wasn't so good at the dress-up part, but I excelled at the drunken lunches and parties.

It was after a party—I was with a group of high school friends who had also landed in Ottawa, which was the closest big city to the valley I grew up in—that I bullied two women. It was late, and the women were walking towards us on the sidewalk. One of the guys yelled, "Hey look at the fuckin' lezzies holding hands!"

We all started taunting them: "Hey, are you fuckin' queers? Yeah you, you fuckin' dykes. A couple of freaks. Homo losers."

When we got up on them, the couple stepped off the concrete walkway and bunched together, heads down, ignoring our insults. It was dark, the area was isolated, and we were feral in our attack. Fear flared from their huddle and filled the space between us. I could smell it, the sharp and tangy pheromones, and I knew it was wrong. But I didn't stop. Guilty.

The encounter shook me, and through it, I was made to look in the mirror where my likenesses to Bev were exposed and raw. The image didn't match the carefree kid in a dirty t-shirt making a spectacular save during a street hockey game. I carried the ache for months because I couldn't find the words or the language to understand my poor behaviour. I became sad and lethargic. Then one day, on a benign errand with a friend, I unexpectedly blurted, "I think I'm gay." The relief was instantaneous. I was free and ready for a new start. Sometime later, I quit my secretarial gig and enrolled in a machine shop course.

Ottawa became a new world to me. The Coral Reef nightclub was a cave-like room; it was twenty-one steps below street level underneath the Rideau Centre's parking garage. Open since the late '60s, it had started life as a Caribbean dance club. It became a mixed gay bar when the Latin clientele moved on after discovering it was open to the queer community on some nights. Homer, the club owner and manager, offered two nights a week for women only on Thursdays and Fridays. It was the place—actually it was the only place in Ottawa at the time—

for gay women, lesbians, and those in-between or curious looking to dance and socialize. The club was also affectionately referred to as the Oral Grief, and I spent countless hours there dancing, drinking, laughing, crying, and occasionally grinding crotches to disco dance anthems such as "Born to Be Alive" and "That's the Way I Like It."

In the early '80s, lesbian communities were intimate, and everyone pretty much knew everyone else, or knew someone who knew someone you wanted to know. We all seemed to know when someone new was in town. A friend, who was into lesbian sadomasochism, described the dating scene at the time as incestuous. She explained that our population was small and that those who were not publicly out made it even smaller, limiting partner selections. She wasn't wrong. The pitcher on my softball team had been with the catcher before being with the right fielder, who had been with the catcher before the coach; the coach was with the first base, who had at one time shared spit with one of the fielders—I don't remember which one. I believed there may be a section in the *Lesbian Handbook* that described this phenomenon, along with other enduring lesbian practices such as moving in with each other on the second date and how to remain friends with all your exes.

Coming out and finding my team gave me a safe place, some new words, and a community where I belonged. I was generally happy even though Bev's legacy, the butch tag, still percolated. I stuffed it away and instead proudly described myself as a dyke, an early reclamation of the insult that made most of my gay women friends cringe and look away. I quickly sorted out the people I could use the descriptor with (not many) and the people I couldn't (too many).

My butch phobia deepened in the '90s when I took a women's studies course at Carleton University. During a class gathering, I overheard a conversation between two lesbian feminists about the need for women to have equality, equal pay, recognition for unpaid work like childcare and homecare, and how unproductive it was for lesbians to play the male role in same-sex relationships. This gender modelling, they claimed, only perpetuated the male hierarchy and its continued dominance over women. They might as well have slapped me with their Birkenstocks. The notion of buying a dildo to play with in my current relationship fizzled and died—suddenly, it was dead, stomped on, never to rise again.

I can't specifically point to a day or a time or even a moment when I decided to come out in my forties as butch. It was more like a prolonged opening of the closet door, a process that allowed me to safely shed the final strands of my bias and to acknowledge the perpetuations and lies of my false self, the one I constructed to protect myself and please others. From the moment I was born, my butch self didn't have a chance. It dissolved when my parents and society shaped and shamed me into becoming their version of myself. Domestication.

Unravelling their will and influence gave me a happy, deep confidence I'd never known. And the bonus was that I finally got to meet the person I had been avoiding for over thirty years, a butch with her own chain wallet.

Some people in the community have said my being butch was a way of acting out my unfulfilled need to transition to the male gender. It wasn't. I was happy being a woman, even though I wasn't that thrilled with how lengthy my breasts had become. They could have gone, but Paula liked them.

As for the dildo play, I had no desire to take on the male anatomy and its accompanying baggage. I was reminded of a scene in the 1985 film *Desert Hearts*, where the free-spirited lesbian Cay was asked, "How do you get all that traffic with no equipment?" Well, if someone needs to inquire...

With self-confidence and mindfulness, the slurs and hateful words of my adolescence had vanished from my person, leaving spaces that were filled with love and respect, light and peace, awareness and intentions.

* * *

Since my teens, words had also been reclaimed and reassembled to describe my community. The classic terms—*lesbian, gay, bisexual,* and *transgender*—had become part of a fluid list that included *ally, androgynous, asexual, bi-gender, butch, cisgender, cissexual, dyke, fag, faggot, femme, gender queer, gender neutral, homo, intersexed, non-binary, omnisexual, pansexual, pangender, queer, questioning, tranny, transfolk, transgenderist, transsexual,* and *Two Spirit*.

I wonder what word Bev would choose at this time to call me. I can't ask her because she has left this world, but I know in my heart she would have still picked butch. It was predetermined. In the way only a mother knows her daughter, she knew it to be me.

During a recent discussion about self-identifying on the spectrum, my friend Sharp described themself as butch and non-binary, existing outside the binary on a circle where the male and female genders are on opposing points. I would add another dimension to this image. I saw a globe where the male and female binaries are like hands holding a ball, fingers blending and shading outward before gradually disappearing towards the non-binary equator.

I saw my spot. It had always been there for me to stand in. For me and my chain wallet, my jeans, my boots, my tattoos, and my Harley.

CHAPTER 7
NEVER TO BE

YELLOWSTONE NATIONAL PARK was yellow, as advertised. I entered the park late enough to avoid the morning lineups—which they still had in mid-September, beyond the high tourist season—but early enough to get the last available campsite at the Indian Creek Campground.

I unpacked my Ford Edge and organized my food and cooler in the large, bear-proof, heavy-duty steel box. Its steel-tube legs were cemented into a small pad near the entrance. Every site had a sign that insisted campers follow the food storage and handling rules: don't leave food out on tables or in tents, dispose of garbage in assigned containers, and do not wash or rinse your dishes at the water stations.

I thought about setting up my tent to sleep in, but it would mean emptying the car and dismantling my sleeping set-up. I'd gotten a whiff of myself when I was loading the bear box, so I decided that time was better spent looking for a shower or bath.

There were no shower facilities at Indian Creek, so I grabbed a bag and stuffed it with a towel, soap, clean underwear, socks, and a t-shirt and headed out into the bush to find the creek.

On the day I left Hinton, south of Jasper, Alberta, I pulled off the highway and followed a sketchy trail down to the Athabasca River. The water was fast-moving and clear, touched lightly with a drop of turquoise dye. I picked my way through the brush along the water to where there was an eddy, a calm area hidden from the cars speeding along the road.

When I sat down on the gravel riverbed, the glacial water came up over my shoulders. Every part of me, my nipples mostly, was telling me to get out. Against my free will, I stayed immersed, spectacularly cold and shivering, and temporarily hypnotized by the power and brilliance of the mountains—the snow resting on chiselled caps and ledges, the cloudy mists settling between the peaks, the many blues of the sky. After a few minutes, I was brought back to my senses by how damn cold the water was, and made some shivering attempts with a slippery bar of soap before making my way back to shore.

The water of Indian Creek was just as cold and refreshing, but the soft muddy bottom close to shore wasn't nearly as nice as the gravel bed of the Athabasca. Clean and refreshed, I stood naked and towelled myself off in a trampled clearing beside the water. I looked around and saw the beaten-down foliage of nearby critter trails.

Fear spiked up from my gut when I realized I had broken most, if not all, of the bear country safety rules of the park. I was alone; I didn't have a whistle or a deterrent like bear spray; and on my way to the creek, I was walking around, exploring the bush and daydreaming, not paying attention or making any of the noise the rangers suggested you do while walking through dense vegetation.

I dressed as fast as a person could pull on dry clothing over damp skin, and I started back to the campsite. I supposed there were worse ways to leave this world than being mauled to death by a grizzly in Yellowstone.

The one rule I was easily able to follow on my way back to my site was *Do Not Run*. It was important to move slowly because, as the poster advised, bears have an instinct to chase.

Once I was safely back in the campground, I relaxed my stride, slowed my breathing, and tried to unfurrow my brow.

I stopped to look at a Yamaha 600 that was all geared up with boxes, bags, and some custom tubes mounted above the exhaust on one side. The licence plate was not one I recognized.

"Yes, that's mine."

I turned towards the voice. It belonged to a lean man dressed in boots, jeans, and several layers of shirts—I saw a turtleneck, a t-shirt, a shirt, and a jacket—walking towards me. "Hi, I'm Graham." We shook hands.

Graham, from Britain, was on the twenty-seventh month of a four-year trip around the world. He said he was waiting for his wife to retire. He was sixty-seven, and she was several years younger. He had his bike shipped from Russia to Halifax in April. It was minus ten degrees Celsius when he landed on the east coast. He rode up and down while crossing Canada and then as far north as he could, exploring the Dalton Highway up to the Arctic Ocean.

"Do you ever see your wife?" I asked.

"Every six months, she flies to where I am for a few weeks to visit."

He told me his plan was to drive down to Argentina and then have his bike shipped to Africa. Graham was uncertain about riding through the continent because of the unstable conditions and unrest within several countries. He was still "mulling over" his southern hemisphere plans.

We shook hands again. "All the best, man, and keep your rubber down."

The next morning Graham was gone.

I drove the outer loop of the park counter to the clock and saw plumes of smoke rising up from the land through fumaroles, vents in the earth's crust that emit steam and volcanic gases. I visited roaring mountains, lakes, hot springs, and Old Faithful.

I stopped at the gift store in the large and spacious Old Faithful complex and, after browsing, picked up a book—*The Last Indian War* by Elliot West. It promised me an unforgettable portrait of the Nez Perce War of 1877.

The stampede of settlers into their traditional territories, sparked by the discovery of gold, caused eight hundred Nez Perce, including women, children, and the elderly, to flee across fifteen hundred miles before stopping mere miles from the safety of Sitting Bull's camp in Canada.

Chief Joseph, one of the last leaders of the Nez Perce—also known as the Nimiipuu, or "the real people"—surrendered after five months, saying, "From where the sun now stands, I will fight no more forever."

The clerk at the store helped me convert my Yellowstone Pass to a National Park Pass. "You'll be able to access all parks for a year," he said. He rang through the book. "Aaaahhh, Chief Joseph. Good choice. Would you like a bag?"

The schedule for Old Faithful was displayed on an inner wall of the complex. It was an expected twenty-five minute wait for it to spout. Not far from the schedule was a plaque that described a Shoshone belief: *The earth is more alive where geysers and hot boiling water is present. Because of its geyser basins and thermal areas, Yellowstone is considered to have a lot of medicine and be a powerful spiritual place.*

I tracked a straight run out to the viewing area and sat down on an aluminum bench. With the exception of a few couples milling about and wandering along the walkways in the distance, I was alone. After a few minutes, not feeling the spirit of the geyser, I got up and left.

Leaving Yellowstone Lake, I drove into a slowdown. Orange cones and yellow placards were set up to slow traffic. Packs of people huddled in small groups on the right side of the road, and a scattering of rangers, wearing yellow traffic vests, were directing cars to slow down but to keep moving through the area.

It was impossible to count the number of tripods, cameras, binoculars, and equipment bags that were strewn behind photographers. Some cameras had lenses as long as a decent bouquet of roses for a first date—not that I've ever received or wanted one, but I've seen enough to size them up.

The people were all looking across the road in the same direction. I could feel the excitement and tension; it crackled in their movement and chatter. I had to veer left so I wouldn't run over the toes of a couple sitting close to the road. Later I learned the cause of the frenzy was the sighting of a wolf pack ranging in the area. The crowd had assembled in anticipation the pack would travel over the bluff towards them.

It was late afternoon when I got back to camp, and I quickly threw some salad, tomatoes, cottage cheese, and tuna into a bowl. I started a fire and ate the mix straight from the bowl, staring into the flames, the sights of the day coming back like slides ratcheting through a projector.

When the light dimmed, it was cold enough that I had to stand and turn my back to the fire to warm my torso and legs. After a few minutes, I rotated back to face the warmth, not quite a spinning top, more like a slow-motion shawarma spit.

I had reached an elevation of over seven thousand feet, and I expected the Indian River would be just as cold that evening as it was the night before. It was minus two degrees Celsius, according to my Ford. I wore sweats to bed and had to cocoon in my sleeping bag to get warm enough to drift off to a night of restless sleep. I tried to indulge my nightly habit of reading but gave up when my arms got too cold from protruding out of the sleeping bag. I cursed myself again for not picking up the Pendleton blanket I had drooled over at a shop in Livingston.

On my third day, I left early in the morning, heading out the northeast exit of the park through fields with herds of bison. The day before, I'd come across a massive beast sunning itself twenty feet from the road. I stopped to take its picture while staying out of sight behind the Edge, adrenalin making my heart thump and hands shake. Last year a woman was badly hurt when taking a selfie with a bison. The ungulate charged, she ran, but the beast caught up to her and tossed her into the air. I imagined the effortless flicking off of an annoying mosquito.

Yellowstone was its own world and ecosystem; its uniqueness and natural wonders were alluring, and I heeded the call to leap in and explore, leaving blessed with gifts. The park's steam and hot springs, ancient layers of yellow stone, gullies and valleys, and canyon falls were truly spectacular and magnificent. I saw an osprey, bison, wolves, an eagle, and a mama bear with her cub. I even had a friendly encounter with a raven looking for a handout. It was beautiful and amazing, a place I'd bring Paula to visit. I texted her a picture of the falls on my second day of exploring, hinting about visiting together in the future, but she hadn't responded.

I blamed my sleeplessness on being cold—and it was likely partially to blame—but not hearing from her had been niggling at me. *Does she want out? Is she afraid to tell me?*

I tuned the radio. The protests at Standing Rock had been in the news almost every day, and I just learned Obama had called a halt to the construction of the pipeline. I thought about how incredible it would be to visit the camp. *Maybe, maybe not.*

My mind shifted quickly, back to the unfolded map and the Black Hills of South Dakota. Being a Harley rider, I've always dreamed of visiting the mecca of motorcycle culture, Sturgis.

* * *

I tried to be a loyal secretary. I really did. I had the hemorrhoid to prove it. Or so I thought. One morning I saw the bright red blood-stained toilet paper after I did my business in a stall at work, and since I'd never engaged in anal sex, a hemorrhoid was the only explanation I could come up with.

Asking my work colleagues was not an option. We were not close enough to discuss our asses, and since it was 1979, I couldn't exactly Google it on my smartphone while sitting on the porcelain throne. When I looked back into the stall, I saw the hemorrhaging as a symbol of my commitment, at the time, to sitting in a chair for the rest of my life working as a secretary.

In high school, I was shuttled into the girls' path and made to take shorthand, typing, business correspondence, and home economics. I didn't want to take those classes, but I didn't have a choice. It was Eric's decision. If I had been able to choose, I would have taken all the shop classes—auto, welding, wood, and machining—and art classes, lots of them.

Instead of learning how to set the table for when my future husband came home after work for his dinner of meat and potatoes, lovingly cooked by my own two hands, I might have instead been cleaning and greasing front wheel bearings, arc welding steel, brazing cast iron, turning metal or wood blanks on a lathe, or creating beautiful pieces of art that would inspire me for a lifetime.

It wasn't to be. I could only dream of those things while I sat transcribing *Alice in Wonderland* in shorthand class. This wasn't to say I wasn't committed to doing my best in my business classes. The opposite was true—I was top of my classes, achieving certificates for 80 words a minute in typing and 120 words a minute in Pitman shorthand. I cherished those skills later, but I didn't as much then. I never really connected with Alice or fully understood the story of her adventures.

I saw the transcriptions and typing practices as required chores to get a job. My work until then had meant shovelling snow, delivering papers, and occasionally babysitting. Office skills would help me get real employment. All I needed to do was graduate school and leave town.

My mom gave me twenty dollars to start my new work life, and I hitchhiked to Ottawa with all my belongings in one suitcase. It was mid-June of 1977, and by the first week of July, I had my first job. It was as a SCY 1, a secretary for Metric Commission Canada, an agency of the government that oversaw the transition from the imperial system to the metric system. My starting salary was $7,443.00, a big number for a girl who shovelled driveways for two dollars a snowfall, an amount I split with my brother Craig. I wasn't considered an adult when I was hired, so I had to wait five months until I was eighteen years old for all the deductions, like the Canada Pension Plan, to be taken off my pay cheque.

While the job didn't provide any deep meaningful personal connection, it was incredibly empowering for me to make and pay my own way in the world. It gave me independence and freedom from my meagre beginnings.

But, like all things not in line with your inherent spirit, it wouldn't last. I didn't fit in a job where you were encouraged to dress like a girl, wear makeup, and flirt with the bosses (who were all men). I didn't have the confidence to tell anyone I was likely gay, and dressing like a girl made me feel horrible. I felt I had to put in my time. I gave it the best I could, and quitting after two years and one hemorrhoid qualified as a genuine effort. Even though my director insisted I was leaving a "for life" government job for the unknown, I knew I had to leave. There was something better out there for me. I felt it. That summer, I got a job washing dishes at Jasper Park Lodge.

I was originally hired as a housekeeper, but after a week of cleaning rooms, I told my supervisor I had a bad knee. It wasn't an excuse to get out of the work. Cleaning toilets, vacuuming, and emptying the odd puke bucket didn't bother me. It was the isolation. I was lonely and wanted to be with people. He admonished me for not disclosing an injury that would prevent me from doing the job I was hired for and said the only opening he had available was as a dishwasher. I hung my head in fake shame, hiding my grin, and told him, "sorry, I thought it wouldn't be a problem. Washing dishes will be fine."

I worked the late shift with a crew of up to eight people, depending on events and which restaurants were open. The supervisor was a fat German man. He always dressed in kitchen whites and very rarely did anything other than sit at his desk in the corner of the kitchen, eating and reading. On most days, he'd chew on raw bacon, his red cheeks seeming to heave up and down with the effort. He always left at the end of day shift around five o'clock, usually without a word.

My shift started at three o'clock in the afternoon, and several times a week, he would tell me to come and sit with him. He'd offer me bacon, and inevitably he'd ask me to join him in his room for drinks after my shift. I'd protest meekly that there was work to be done and I should be on the line instead of sitting. Two weeks later, he made me a supervisor, and I could sit with him longer. I felt obligated to do as he said, so I obediently sat in the chair. I asked him questions and engaged in conversations I didn't fully understand because of his accent. He off-gassed old grease and disinfectant—we all did after being in the kitchen for a shift.

After a few days, I made an ongoing arrangement with a crew member to come over and get me when I was with him. They would say there was a problem with a machine or a backlog with pots, or they couldn't find the solution for soaking the silverware.

There was continuous pressure from the fat German. The insistence I go to his room intensified every day. I offered up lots of excuses and started to hide in other parts of the kitchen. I even found work in the sister restaurants, eluding him until I knew his shift was over. After a couple of weeks of successful avoidance, I came in to find a new employee sitting in my chair. She was pretty and slim and sat in an awkward way with her hands all twisted up in her kitchen apron. She was chewing bacon. I felt relief.

Work in the kitchen was hard and hot. One busy night we were all giddy with relief after several intense rushes. The quiet time after a frenzied shift. We were relieved to be done for the night with the knowledge there wouldn't be another busboy loaded with dirty dishes and cutlery coming our way after kicking the door open. A prep cook came over and offered up a bag of buns. The first bun came zipping by my head within seconds, and the ensuing food fight got our competitive adrenalin pumping. We scattered and took cover behind the stacks of equipment and stainless-steel counters, shrieking and yelling. Leftovers scraped from plates and food pulled from the garbage cans joined the airborne buns. The fight was over in minutes, even though it felt like longer. We stood in a circle, breathing heavily, leaning over with our hands on our knees and laughing, our whites and aprons stained and wet, already talking trash about who got who and whose hair was full of gravy and mashed potatoes and bits of Yorkshire pudding.

While I had a blast being part of the kitchen crew and I worked hard on shift, I was the target of violence at the lodge when I was off one evening. I reacted badly.

The jobs at Jasper during the high season were mostly summer positions filled by students and young people looking for an adventure out west. We drank a lot, and one night a guy from the landscaping and maintenance crew looked at me strangely, his eyes narrowed and mean. "What the fuck you looking at?" he said.

I replied sarcastically, "Nothing much." I turned to a friend and laughed. "What's this asshole's problem?"

The moment I looked back at him, he swung at me. "Fucking lezzie bitch." His fist connected with the side of my face, and I staggered backwards, fell over a chair and landed heavily on the wooden floor.

One of his buddies pulled him back. "What the fuck, man?"

A couple of my friends from the kitchen helped me up and yelled at his crowd to get him the "fuck away."

I was familiar with violence, and physical fights in my family were common. We learned that beating each other up was how we got what we wanted and that if you were the winner, you weren't the loser. And no one wanted to be the loser.

Angry, I shook off my friends and spent the rest of the night drinking tequila, plotting, watching the landscaper guy, and waiting. When the time came, I walked up behind him and tapped him on the shoulder. When he turned to face me, I swung my bottle of beer as hard as I could, connecting with his head. He fell to the floor. I won. His buddies stood open-mouthed in shock, and I could hear others repeating, "Holy fuck." They were trying to help him up when I walked out.

I woke up with a bruised face—I couldn't open my mouth fully—and a kind of hangover I'd never experienced before. I haven't had tequila since. There were some things I was very grateful for in my life, and one of them was that the landscaper guy was okay. There were so many ways it could have turned out badly for both of us. A couple of days later, I saw him walking to one of the machine sheds. He looked up, recognized me, and quickly put his head down, accelerating his pace along the gravel path.

* * *

At the end of the summer, I left Jasper for Vancouver and spent a couple of weeks immersed in the lesbian culture scene before flying home. While looking for work pumping gas, I applied for a machine shop retraining program through the government-backed Manpower Training Program. I was thrilled to be accepted, even though it meant I had to move closer to Brockville. St. Lawrence College didn't have a machine shop, so our class was bussed to Seaway District High School in Iroquois to use its facilities after school had finished for the day.

I was enamoured with the shop from the first day I stepped into the space. It felt like home. I ran my hand over the workbenches, turned the vice handles, and stood in front of the machines and equipment, trying to decipher their purpose and workings. I came to love the smell of oil and cutting fluid. I even loved how the small metal filings would blacken my hands and fingers, a sign of being a working woman.

Our first project was to square up a small steel block, the size of a large bar of soap, by using hand files and a small square. Once it was square, we drilled a hole close to an edge and removed the remaining material by hand using a chisel and a hammer. We created a channel using the hole as the bottom of the u-shape.

I happily filed, chiselled, checked square and tolerances, and polished the block for hours. I wasn't alone in my happiness, but there were others in our class who were not interested or motivated enough to work a metal block by hand. One guy, in particular, complained steadily: "This is bullshit, man. It's called machine shop, not hand shop." It got so bad that no one wanted to share a bench with him. From a distance, you could see his block was a wreck—it wasn't even close to meeting tolerances—and I know several of us would have helped him if he'd have asked and stopped his ranting about the project being so unfair. Eventually, his continuous vitriol caused a push back. "Shut the fuck up," became a common response, repeated several times over by a number of us, myself included.

Someone had taken to bringing in a radio, and the first ones into the shop clustered around it, trying to ignore him. Finally, one day after two weeks into the course, he slammed the block down on the workbench. "This is just fucking bullshit. I'm done!" There was a cheer when he walked out.

Another culling of a classmate came soon after. I was laying out measurements and centre punching for some drilling work when someone ran past me and grabbed the fire extinguisher off the wall. He pulled the pin and blasted the hose into a large garbage bin on wheels. A minute later, our instructor Rod boomed, "Everyone in the classroom. NOW!" Rod was a mild-mannered man, originally from England. With his reddish-brown hair, goatee, and wire-rimmed glasses, he gave the impression of an eccentric intellectual. He was kind but firm, and he expected all of us to pay attention, learn, and give our best effort as we were being paid by Manpower to attend class.

"What the hell do you think you were doing?" he yelled while looking at two guys who were sitting in the back row with their heads down. "What were you thinking?" he shouted again, his voice shaking. One guy, a loner who smoked by himself during breaks, spoke first: "What's the problem, man? It was just a fucking mouse." He and the guy sitting beside him, who still had his head down, had found a mouse in the garbage bin. They had poured oil on some paper towels and shoved them into the bin, trapping the mouse. The loner lit the paper on fire and with it, the mouse.

The other guy finally lifted his head. He was crying and said, "I'm sorry." The loner shook his head at him and looked around at the rest of us, putting his palms up: "What the fuck! We were just having a little fun, and it was just a fucking mouse." I was horrified and speechless, as most of us were, and over the next week, the loner and head-hanger were shunned and avoided. The head-hanger apologized continuously until someone told him to shut up. The loner sneered at us, and the tension in the shop was palpable. It deflated when he went on longer and longer smoke breaks. One day he never came back. It took a couple of days of his absence before our group collectively sighed with relief.

Eventually, the head-hanger left as well. We gradually included him, became his project partners again, and helped him out where we could, but his demeanour had deflated. After "mousegate," it seemed his heart was never in the work.

While he disappeared, my passion for the shop never abated. I studied the books and machine manuals and worked on the shop floor. One day we were tested on how to calculate the machining of gears using an indexing attachment on a milling machine. We had to calculate the number of turns required on the index for certain diameters and the number of gears before machining to depth. It was a theory test that used a complicated formula, and I was the only one who passed. I even got a perfect score. I was pissed that Rod dismissed the marks and used the test as a practice assignment instead. We were given a new test a few days later, and the rest of the class, with a few exceptions, passed.

I have come to understand his approach, even though I didn't at the time. It wasn't the fault of my classmates that they didn't understand the task; it was a failure of the teaching and learning methodology. But I was still pissed.

* * *

During the training program, I had my first of many memorable bathroom moments. My classmates and I wore coveralls, both as a layer of personal protection and to keep our street clothes clean. One afternoon I went into the girls' bathroom wearing mine. There were two teenagers at the sinks, both dressed in shorts, wearing sneakers. I assumed they were engaged in some after-school practice of some sort like basketball or volleyball. I walked into a stall, and the laughing started with a shriek from one: "Omigod, he's in the wrong washroom!" I heard them run out, giggling and gasping. I was embarrassed and waited in the stall until I was confident they wouldn't be lurking out in the hall, waiting to make fun of me. Afterwards, whenever I went to the washroom, I'd remove the top part of my coveralls and tie the empty sleeves around my waist, hoping any girls I'd see would recognize I had breasts like them.

I also found it helpful to arch my back thrusting out my tits before entering any women's washroom. Some days it worked, others not so much.

When we were nearing the end of our course in the spring, most of us gathered outside during our breaks at picnic tables bunched together on the grounds. We smoked, compared test scores, teased each other, and shared project tips. Most often, I found myself chatting with Rick, a hard-working guy who was sharp, smart, and optimistic about finding a job after school ended in a month.

One afternoon he said, "I'll drive you anywhere in the province you want to go."

I looked at him, confused. "What?"

He clarified. "Yeah, I'll drive you anywhere you want to go as long as it's out of town."

Confused and disappointed because I thought we were friends, I replied, "Okay, not sure what that's about."

He looked over at a couple of guys who were listening in, before he turned back and said, "It's because I don't want to compete with you for a job around here."

I initially thought he was joking, and when he repeated his offer a few more times later in the week, I told him to shut it.

If I could have, I would have stayed longer than the forty-two weeks the course took to complete. The last mandatory component was work experience. Rod pulled me aside into his office, closed the door, and said that he had problems finding me a placement because I was a girl. "I've called in a favour and should have some news for you in the next couple of days." Two days later, on a Thursday, he told me my work experience, starting Monday, was going to be in the tool and die shop at the Black & Decker plant in Brockville.

I showed up an hour early. The complex felt huge, and the machine shop was spacious and busy, infused with the now familiar smell of oil and metal. I was intimidated but excited. My first job was to mill out a cavity in a block that would be used as one-half of a mould.

I'd been given a tour of the plant, where I saw the heavy blocks rotating on a plastic injection machine. They came together to make one half of a plastic drill casing. There were six moulds, made up of six halves, all identical.

It was rough, imprecise work using a top-of-the-line milling machine with a carbide cutter. I took instructions from the shop foreman to set the speed, depth, and feed of the cutter and started milling. The shavings came off bright red, and to prevent burns, I stood behind a clear plexiglass shield. I also had to set the automatic feed stops, but I was afraid to let it go, not wanting to damage the machine or the cutter if it jammed into the end. This fear meant reaching out from behind the shield to stop the feed, finishing the end cuts manually. The pattern became reach, sizzle, reach, sizzle. After an hour, the tops of my hands looked like I had chicken pox, and it was painful to put my hands into the pockets of my jeans. Despite the discomfort, I was happy for the praise I received with the finished rough mould cavity.

I was thrilled to be in the shop, content with drilling holes and roughing out moulds. During breaks, I would visit the benches of the tool and die makers, some of whom came from England, and wondered at their ability to create beautiful compound curved parts and pieces by hand. I was sad when the week ended.

After lunch on the last day, the men in the shop came together and presented me with a Black & Decker Workmate and the highest praise, a lament from the foreman: "If it was in my budget, I'd hire you tomorrow."

His lament became my optimism, my "I'm going to prove you wrong" mantra, and it carried me through the shops I visited looking for a job as an apprentice machinist.

"Why do you want to work here? It's dirty."

"I can't hire you—my wife would kill me."

"You'd be a distraction for the men."

My friend Rick needn't have worried about my competing with him for a job in the area. It was never to be.

The pay from Manpower helped with rent and food, but not much more. To help support myself through school, I worked part-time at a small body shop prepping and sanding cars. If I couldn't find work in a machine shop, how about a body shop?

CHAPTER 8
BROTHERS

NORTHERN WYOMING was as magnificent as Yellowstone. The beauty of the mountains and high plains along the Chief Joseph Scenic Byway left me speechless, in a wondrous awe. I couldn't do them justice. Sadly, what little tools I had in my literary box were woefully not up for the task. The passes and plains have rooted a desire to return and fully explore this exceptional country.

I drove south into Cody, east to Greybull, and then southeast to Ten Sleep. A fairly large sign—white with faded blue capital letters—explained that the town got its name after the Indian method of measuring distance, being halfway or "ten sleeps" between two Indian camps. The bottom of the sign shows three pictograms: two hands and a teepee.

The radio voices of the Midwest were mostly religious, farming ones, laser focused on broadcasting ultra-conservative views with its stranglehold on what defines family. I listened to Turning Point, whose mission was to deliver the unchanging Word of God. Since entering Montana, I had learned about Obama's hostility towards Christians in what they called a religious war on their faith, rights, and cultural divinity. I heard ads for treatments of ulcers in horses, and I listened to a deep voice, calming and strong, talking about the Clear Choice Clinic offering life-affirming reproductive healthcare for men and women. I learned about a Christian conservative organization called Vision America. I heard infomercials selling the appeal of only needing thirty days to make better choices, to call them, and commercials claiming that "God allows pain to humble us."

Lastly, I learned about "Genie God," a convenient, quick-fix mindset in which you only invoke the Almighty "when you need him." In the spirit of sharing, my revelation and latest confession is that, yes, I have called on the Genie God at inconvenient times—mostly on Saturday nights and Sunday mornings, and the occasional Monday, maybe Tuesday, too.

I backed into a space in a nicely wooded picnic area just west of Moorcroft to spend the night. I was joined by a couple of cars and two trucks pulling trailers. There was a small building with washrooms, and I quickly stepped in and out to get ready for bed. It was chilly and awkward getting in and out of my sleeping bag, and then in and out of the rear passenger side door of the Edge. This quickly taught me to not drink any water past six o'clock if I didn't want to have to get up in the middle of the night to squat sleepily in some nearby bushes or the back of a dark building.

It was a restless and scary night. I dreamt about an arm reaching through the side window. It tried to smother me, cupping my mouth. After I kept pushing it away, it wrapped its long fingers around my neck, choking off my breath. I managed to twist the arm and bite it as hard as I could. I woke up to a woman's screams, breathing hard, convinced there was someone outside the car trying to get in.

Uneasy and awake, I pushed myself upright; the Ford bounced slightly. It was dark, and I swept my hand slowly across the top of the cooler. My hand found the key fob, and I double-clicked the lock icon. The locks engaged with a loud clunk of metal on metal and two beeps of the horn. I rolled back, pulled up the edges of the sleeping bag and tried to quiet the thumping rush of heartbeats sounding off in my chest and head.

Would I have felt safer if Paula were with me? It's kind of a moot question because there's no doubt she would never sleep in a car, and she would never squat in anything with less than porcelain to sit on and a door to close. I'd have to invest in a motorhome or travel trailer. Around mid-day yesterday, she responded to my text about the falls. She said *Beautiful*, and followed it up with, *I'd love to see them in person one day.* I'm not certain if she means alone. I wouldn't blame her after our Mark blowout.

***

"Mark's in town," I told Paula. She was washing dishes and kept her head down. The sound of clinking dishes and running water consumed the space between us.

"We're going to meet up with John and Alex at the restaurant."

Paula wrung out the dishrag and turned to wipe down the counter.

"Here we go again. Every time I mention Mark or John, you shut down and turn away."

Paula turned to face me. "They don't deserve you. Look at Mark. He ignored you for almost fifteen years. How is that okay? How is that right?"

"Fuck, we've been through this. It's not your problem to own. It's mine." I complained.

Paula's expression turned hard. "It is my problem because I've been the one that's been here for you all these years. He hasn't, and now you want it to be all okay and let him show up in your life, like nothing has happened."

Angry, I got louder, "We keep having the same conversation over and over. I'm not doing this anymore. You don't give a fuck about anybody but yourself."

"That's unfair, and it's not true."

I stepped towards Paula, tremors clenching my gut. Without thinking, I pointed and yelled, "Really? Really? If I treated your family the way you treat mine, you wouldn't be with me. Would you?"

Paula didn't respond. Instead, she retreated to the sink and lowered her head, looking for dishes under a storm of soap clouds. We were both crying. I left the room.

***

Restless and unable to get back to sleep, I quickly dressed, jammed a ball cap on, and got on the road. It was almost six-thirty in the morning when I picked up a coffee at Donna's Diner. "It's nice to find a place open this early for coffee."

The woman handed me my coffee with a tired smile. "We open every day at four-thirty."

It was too early for a response, but I texted Paula anyway, *Thinking of you*. My resentments had softened like a wax candle sitting in the hot sun—not a lot, but enough that I'm able to lean into the dismantling of my behaviours. Every time I drilled down below my anger, my fear, the result was the same: a child who never believed she would be good enough.

I drove towards the sun lifting off the horizon and landed in Sturgis a couple of hours later. At the McDonald's, where I stopped for a second coffee, was a crew of riders from the Twisted Drifters MC (Motorcycle Club), based out of Sioux Falls, South Dakota. I slipped into a spot beside one rider, a lean, thin, and mean-looking Kid Rock type. He was cutting up a long-sleeved t-shirt with a sharp blade, trying to fashion himself some kind of lower face covering. It might have been to keep his neck and face warm but seeing him slash at the cloth between fittings, it could have been to amp up his biker image instead.

There was a custom piece of art on his tank inspired by the Second Amendment, an oval with a skeleton in the middle surrounded by text: *You can have my gun when you pry it from my cold dead hands.* His partner wore a headband that shouted SICK BITCH across her forehead. Sparkles and gems embellished her jeans, and her off-white leather purse, which she had slung over one shoulder, was covered with shiny rivets.

He yanked the fabric down around his neck and stretched it up over his nose. Satisfied, he pulled it over his head and stowed it in a jacket pocket, and they walked together holding hands into the McDonald's. I followed them and took my coffee to go.

I found some space in the corner of the parking lot near a park with a large garbage can. I drained my cooler and then cleaned out the Edge, where receipts, used napkins, empty coffee cups, and pop cans had accumulated. I organized my laundry, fluffed my pillows, and shook out my sleeping bag before covering it with a new Pendleton blanket I picked up at the Yellowstone Trading Post in Cooke City. Plain grey with stripes, it was going to be a good travelling companion.

My first stop of the day was the Sturgis Harley-Davidson. The only unique feature that made it any different from the numerous other Harley-Davidson shops I had visited was the space reserved out front for picture taking. Orange-painted curbs delineated a section reserved specifically for taking photos in front of the store. I asked a couple leaving the showroom if they could take mine.

Paula replied, *Me too.* The text came after I called to get her advice about buying my sister-in-law Kathy a Harley t-shirt. All the women's clothing was way too girlie to have inspired my inner sense of style. Out of desperation—and let's confess, a desire to hear her voice—I called Paula for help. It had been weeks since we'd talked, and for a moment, I considered hanging up for fear she wouldn't pick up, as was her habit early on in our conflict. When she answered, "This is a nice surprise," I smiled and blushed, happily awkward that she couldn't see my reaction. We quickly settled into an easy back-and-forth banter, talking about Sturgis and Harley, interrupted by my sending her pictures of the tops I was considering for Kathy. We settled on something light and purple with filigree-like graphics and sparkling embellishments. Nervous about saying goodbye, I blurted, "I'll see ya when I see ya."

Encouraged by our talk, I went back to one of the racks of t-shirts that Paula called pretty and picked out one that would fit her. I left the Harley store thinking about taking her for a ride in the future, and if it was too cold, I knew just how to make some quick and easy face protection.

The riding season in South Dakota was over. The nearly half a million people who attended the annual Sturgis Motorcycle Rally in August were long gone, and the streets were bare and quiet. It was also a Sunday, but the shops quietly awakened and opened their doors to the few tourists making the rounds in the later morning.

Sturgis was known as the city of riders, and it had its own small motorcycle museum. I stopped in for a visit and explored the early to mid-century bikes, read about the history of the motorcycle, and saw a significant space devoted to women in motorcycling. I spent more time absorbed in the artefacts, bikes, and photos at the museum than ogling merchandise I couldn't have afforded at the Harley store.

I read about the famous all-female motorcycle clubs—Women in the Wind and Motor Maids—and the inspiring story of Gloria Tramontin-Struck. In 2011, Gloria and Betty Fauls, daughter of the Motor Maids co-founder Dot Robinson, were honoured for sixty-five years of riding. It was also in 2011 that Gloria was inducted into the Hall of Fame at

Sturgis. When she was seventy-four, Gloria and her son shipped their bikes to Europe and conquered the Passo Stelvio pass in the Alps—one of many they rode. Not satisfied, she returned two years later to ride over four thousand miles in eight countries.

An American Motorcycle Association Hall of Famer, now in her 90s, she recently published an autobiography titled *Gloria – A Lifetime Motorcyclist: 75 Years on Two Wheels and Still Riding*. The matriarch of the women's motorcycle community plans to ride cross country for her hundredth birthday in 2025. I imagined Gloria, the motorcycle maiden, followed by lines of women on machines, rumbling and revelling across the nation. Beautiful.

When I left the museum, I walked on top of the Brick Project. A revitalization project for the downtown community, the project had started to replace the sidewalks of the iconic Main Street with engraved brick pavers.

Set level without a discernable pattern, large granite pavers paid tribute to Motor Maids and to the founder of the now-famous rally in Sturgis, JC "Pappy" Hoel and his first lady, Pearl Hoel. A granite marker engraved with *Ready for the Ride, Ready for the Slide* showed a photo of a man standing over a wrecked bike that had obviously crashed.

There were innumerable red bricks engraved with hundreds, if not thousands, of names and dates. These memorials and commemorations were respected by those among us who were still living and riding. It only took a few glances to read the inscriptions which accompanied the names, phrases like: *In Memory of*, *Ride on*, *Ride in the Wind*, *Swamp Mama*, *Harleyman*, *Baboo*, *Bonzai King of the Hill*, *Giddee Up*, *Tigger*, *Ride in Peace*, *Ride Free*, *Spud*, *Butch*, and *Living the Dream*.

I left the pavers with more ghosts than I came with and made my way to an RV park on the edge of town. I drove down Lazelle Street, the main drag where the most iconic photos of the annual rally were taken. I parked in an almost-empty grocery store parking lot across from the Knuckle Saloon, which looked to be a block long. The saloon—along with its rowdy companion, the Iron Horse Saloon—was a prominent landmark, a must-visit for the Sturgis pilgrim.

I've seen the pictures from the exact spot I stood in, and it wasn't difficult for me to envision the sensations and sounds from the exhausts of tens of thousands of motorcycles, the heavy throttles and smoke from the burning tires during brake stands, and the crush of people mingling and partying.

There was no question I would have been fully immersed in the partying on Lazelle at the beginning of my riding life. As a sober older version, if I had the opportunity now, I'd be more inclined to visit the Serenity Club, which held all-day meetings during the annual event. I noticed the club's sign on top of the Integrity Heating and Air Conditioning store on Main Street—it looked like you could attend a meeting and then pick up a needed switch, valve, or filter for your furnace at the same time.

Needing to do some laundry, I drove past the coin-operated laundry, and it was closed. I decided to try the Days End RV Park. RV parks always have laundry facilities. The office was closed. I asked a woman, who was doing laundry in a small brown building with a concrete porch not far from the entrance to the park, if she thought it would be okay if I did some of my own.

Barely glancing at me, with a disinterested shrug of her shoulders, she replied, "Why not?"

I went across the road to the gas station and returned with four dollars in quarters. I loaded eight quarters into the washer, upended my laundry bag, and shook out all my dirty clothes into the washer tub. Paula would have cringed at my thoughtlessness and possible laziness. She was laundry obsessed and sorted loads by colour, type of fabric, type of clothes, temperature, heavy soil, light soil, and so on. Her list was lengthy. At home on a Saturday morning, it wasn't unusual for me to walk by little piles ready to be washed—thongs, light towels, a dark towel, work t-shirts, nice t-shirts, her jeans, my jeans, black socks, grey socks, and assorted other socks depicting a rainbow—the criteria of which I didn't quite understand, nor did I care to.

While I waited for the wash cycle to finish, I sat at a small table in the corner and marked my route up to Sturgis on my maps, indicating which places I had slept in. *Mmmmm, maybe overnighted is a better word?* The hot air in the cramped laundry room carried the tang of burnt soap, and it became quite warm with just the one dryer going, its weight squeaking, a failed bearing or possibly a belt. I wiped my brow using my t-shirt. More laundry.

When the washer stopped spinning, I switched the load to a dryer, jacked in the rest of the quarters, and went around the side of the building to the women's washroom to take a quick shower. I wanted to be cleaned and dressed before the owners got back just in case they weren't happy with an outsider using their facilities.

When I came back round the front, a young boy was sitting on the bench outside the laundromat door. He looked to be about eight years old. His knees and feet were summer dirty, and the faded bike helmet he wore was on backwards. A bicycle was laying in the grass at the edge of the concrete pad of the porch.

My load wasn't quite dry, so I sat back down to explore the map further and see where I might leapfrog next. Acorns flew in through the door, landing with a crack, and then rolled and slid across the floor, stopping at the base of the dryers. I picked them up and went outside to see the boy disappearing around the corner of the building.

Within seconds of settling back at the map, more acorns were tossed onto the floor. The boy and I did this little dance a few times before I stopped responding. It didn't take long before he got up to see if I had somehow disappeared through a non-existent back door before sitting back on the bench.

I went out and sat on the bench beside him. "What's with the acorns?"

He pushed the helmet back on his head, looked down, and rubbed a stain on his shorts. "Nothing."

"Are you waiting for someone?"

"I'm waiting for someone to give me a dollar."

That was smooth. Apparently, the boy had been practising, and I wondered if he even knew what a segue was. *Of course not. He's like eight. And besides, you don't even know how to spell it, so why're you talking?*

He got up and faced the front of the Pepsi machine. Without looking at me, he asked, "Do you have a dollar?"

I paused, not quite sure of his ask, but I guessed there was a lot more going on than asking a stranger for a dollar. I replied, "No, I don't." I suspected I wasn't his first mark or target. "So, how many drinks have you gotten today?"

"Three." He held up his right hand, showing me three fingers. They were sticky with dirt. "One 7-Up and two root beers. I got the 7-Up for my mom. Root beer is my favourite." He smiled at me, making eye contact.

I was being hustled. He reminded me of when Craig and I would clean up after one of Eric and Bev's parties. We tolerated the dirty dishes, pots, and filled ashtrays for the chance to drink real pop like Pepsi or Coke, beverages we were never allowed to have. We'd also eat leftovers, which were also usually treats like bread with real butter, roast beef, or garlic spareribs. If she was happy with how the house looked, Bev would slip us a few bucks each when she'd recovered from her hangover.

Not wanting to encourage him, I waited a few minutes, then walked over to my Ford and rooted through the centre console to see if I could scrape a buck together. While I had my head down, not finding any change regardless of how deep I looked, an old man with two very yappy Shih Tzu dogs on retractable leashes claimed the bench. The kid disappeared but left the bicycle laying on the grass. The old man told me, "They won't bite. They're just loud."

His wife had pushed aside my map, notebook, and pens and was sorting clothes on the table. My load was done, so I pulled my clothes out of the dryer and used the top of a washer to fold them roughly. I packed them into my duffel. I had a clean body with clean clothes and a call with Paula—the day was looking up.

Readied for the road, I decided to backtrack a few miles to Deadwood and drive a loop through the Black Hills, visit the Crazy Horse Monument, possibly drive through Pine Ridge, hopefully visit the Badlands, and then, I didn't know. Maybe Standing Rock on my way home?

I carried my bag, map, and notebook across the worn track in the grass to the Edge. The old man was up and walking the dogs in a field beside the office; they were more pulling him than he was leading the pair.

The boy returned with a dark-haired young man wearing bright surfer shorts and flip-flops. They sat on opposite ends of the concrete pad under the porch in the shade and tossed acorns back and forth between them.

I started the Edge, and for a brief nanosecond, thought about going to get more change at the gas station, but the thought vanished as quickly as it came. My attention was already on Deadwood.

* * *

Hey Craig, I miss you and John. It's difficult for me to believe we've already passed the seventh anniversary of John's death. The years have gone by so quickly, more so now that I'm beyond sixty. Somehow time is accelerating. In our childhood, the end of school seemed to take forever to come; the hours at the beach were endless, hot and decadent; and the wait to go camping along the river was a dream that took its time coming true on Fridays. Is the passage of time the same way for you?

We haven't been the same since John died. I don't think the cause was his death, but rather Mark's appearance back in our lives. We were fine in the years he wasn't around. Or maybe we were just pretending to be a good sister and good brother. Maybe the thing that separated us was inevitable. Is that it?

What has come between us then? I'd like to try and give you my version of what happened, but first, maybe we should find some common ground within our many different views of our history.

We had good and fun times as children. Among them, I think we can agree that the four of us grew up fighting each other fiercely—none of us ever wanted to be on the losing side. We'd see what happened to the loser who fought with Eric, and it would make us do anything to be the winner in our fights. We'd kick, bite, pull hair, and use any other dirty trick we could pull.

What was sad was that we never had the ability to look beyond the fighting. In our immaturity and naivety, we didn't realize the future cost would be periods of estrangement and lack of empathy and compassion for others. We had demonized the other before even knowing what the word meant. We saw each other as barriers, to either jump over or to beat down to get the prize. And we weren't sure what the prize was because we didn't have the language or words to articulate it. I'd say this posturing continues among us today. Let me know if you disagree.

I've acknowledged we learned from the best. Have you? Mom and Eric taught us how to keep secrets, lie, cheat, steal, yell, scream, and beat each other up. We learned to meet every demand, conflict, difficulty, indecision, uncertainty, and fear with anger. In the worst of times, it was raging anger built on a bedrock of resentments. It was how we lived, and we knew it as normal.

There were also the times when we knew we had to run and hide. We learned this pretty quickly too, especially when it was angry Eric coming for us. We weren't always able to get away, and we took the pain and the anger he expressed with his belt and fists and kicks. It created us. His violence made us into anxious, angry, and afraid children. We didn't know how to cope with all the shit raining down on us, so we fought back, tussled with each other, had fights at school, talked back, disappeared, missed school, used, smoked, and drank.

We lived our lives the best way we knew how to survive. And the way was different for each of us. I have come to acknowledge our differences in managing our lives. Have you? Or are you still having difficulty accepting your excessive eating, drinking, lashing out, and negativity as ways to cope and survive the anger in your life?

This is where we would probably disagree. I can recall moments when I've lightly prodded those areas. Remembering how they were met with your dismissal. Your denial was usually phrased in the same way, "Can't you let that shit go?"

Then there were the times when I was harsher and angrier in my poking you, and we always ended up fighting. I couldn't let go of the impact of the violence of our upbringing, but all you wanted to do was forget. Have you ever thought about why you'd rather drink and eat away the pain than face it? Have you ever thought it was because you didn't want to feel?

We both know John didn't want to feel. He spent his life using in some form or another, so he didn't have to make that trip. I was harsh on him. I always told him he had a choice to not drink and to get better, but he really didn't. His first choice before any other was to love himself, but he was never able to get there. Eric made sure of that. And it just wasn't the abuse, the putdowns, the being told we would never be good enough that crushed us. We never had all the good things kids needed to thrive, like holding and affection, reading and storytelling, teaching and learning, trust and responsibility. It has even been difficult to write these words as they seem so foreign to our growing up.

Sure, John got close a couple of times, but something always happened to crack his fragile sobriety, and he'd eventually break. In rehab, we were taught that the recovery process was like riding in an elevator. The basement represented death, the inevitable end of any addict. If you relapsed, you never got back on the elevator at the top floor. You always returned to the floor you got off at when you entered rehab. John was never able to get to the top; he was a tenant on the first floor descending fast. He knew he was going to die before his time, and sadly he didn't care.

Just like you don't care.

That is harsh, isn't it? I know you care about your family, but do you really care that much for yourself? It's been hard to see it if you do. You, Mark, John, and me all chose our own personal brand of vices to help us get along. I used to drink and smoke, and now I can't help binge eating. Every time I get stressed or anxious, I want to stuff a donut in my face, and of course, one leads to a dozen, just like the beer I used to drink.

I know you've felt the same way. I've seen it. You find excuses to drink, eat triple plates at the local buffet, and feed the carb train by indulging in sugar. As a result, you have to wear a breathing machine to sleep. I once suggested maybe your weight was an issue. Your denials were harsh enough that they left no room for me to respond.

I know I have also shut you down during some of our tough conversations. It was how we grew up, remember? Fighting and not letting stuff go. Now, it has been the need to be right that will confirm us as the winner. I know because I—we—do that all the time when we are together.

Paula told me I become a completely different person when I am with my Jorgensen tribe. I have seen it. I begin posturing, working out my place, and then start trouble by bringing up the past and using it to poke people, especially Mark. I haven't been very kind to him. I have trouble with the fact that he hangs on to blaming his ex-wife for him being unavailable and unable to contact us for the years he was absent from our lives. And I let him know just how unhappy I was, instead of trying to understand his circumstances, instead of thinking about *why* he always needs to deflect blame. I wanted him instead on his knees, crying and begging for forgiveness. Of course, that was never going to happen with a Jorgensen. We would never show each other our weaknesses or talk about how raw we are from being so hurt as children. We'd start swinging at each other first.

Have you seen that Mark's way of coping is to drink a lot of wine in bottles with corks—he really is a connoisseur and not a daily drunk—and to over-achieve and then let everyone know how successful he is? His denial and narcissism give me perfect targets.

In one of our last conversations, I told him that his need to continually "pump his own tires" came from a lack of self-esteem and that he should see a therapist.

His response was to take a drink and then poke me back: "Who said that thing once about you being a diesel dyke?"

We are very good at hurting each other. I'm sincere in my hope that we will one day be able to have an adult conversation about real issues, but I doubt it will ever happen.

Mark did what he needed to do to make his way through life. Including trampling people and relatives to get what he wanted or needed to survive. It was the only way he knew how to be. He keeps his life busy and full, and there is no room for any other stuff besides his own. He works excessively, and he's obsessive about filling time—he always has a project or two going, or he's travelling or planning a trip. It's easy to see that, when his life is full, there isn't any space for difficult or emotional conversations or healing.

I've tried in conversations to not blame, to not feel threatened, but I can't seem to be the reasonable one. When I get into a room with the Jorgensen clan, my "who gives a fuck?" bravado comes out, and it's gloves off and glasses up.

I still have a lot of work to do when it comes to Mark.

I wish it wasn't the case, but I still have a lot of work to do when it comes to you as well. I'm not sure you know you've turned into a chronically negative, defeatist, angry man who feeds off conspiracy theories. It's been too much for me, and it was the reason I ended my last visit early. You wanted me to spend another night because there was a snowstorm. I'd stayed for dinner because Morley made ribs as a treat for my visit, but I had to leave. Especially after you called me a "squaw."

Andrew was beside me when you made the loud statement in front of the family, which included your grandchildren. He leaned in and said quietly, "Did he just really say that?"

"Yup." That's when I knew I had to leave. It was only after I stopped for coffee in Mattawa that I realized I'd left my winter jacket at your place. It might still be there on a hook in your mudroom.

Maybe the timing sucked for us to visit. You had just come home from two weeks at a mine in the bush north of Thunder Bay. I get that you were tired and worn out. I know you didn't want to start a new job this late in life, especially one that was fourteen hours from home. Who would? But wasn't it your temper that cost you your last position?

You spent two days in a darkened living room watching TV. I sat with you for a bit, and your derogatory comments about women, your stream of hate, was pretty steady. "Look at the moustache on her."

You wouldn't call it hate, though. You'd call it the truth. You'd say that it wasn't your fault she had a moustache.

We spent some time in the garage, and you were drinking when you started talking about Kathleen Wynne, calling her a "fucking cunt."

It reminded me of the time when you had a few beers on our last motorcycle trip and were making fun of a young boy: "Do you see his tits?"

I called you out both times, and you didn't like it. I didn't like it, it hurt, and it's become impossible for me to be around when you act that way.

When we last talked on the phone, you told me to "stop taking stuff so seriously."

Seriously, am I supposed to give you a free ride and stay silent?

This is why we don't talk now. I don't have the energy to call and have those conversations with you because I know I'd get pissed. We've all had enough anger in our lives.

I've been trying to get better, and I'd like the old Craig back. The loving guy, not the bitter man life has wrung out. You know the guy: the talented teenage hockey player I cheered for, the hero who stood up to Eric because he knew there was a better life, and the friend who slept on the front porch of my apartment waiting for me. That guy.

We had meagre childhoods where not a lot went right. We know that. In fact, a lot went wrong, but it isn't enough to say you are over it. The violence changed us, and we need to open up to it; we need to give it space and time so we can heal it.

Dousing our pain with food, alcohol, denial, and drugs will never work. If you do anything, look at John's death and see our future. I know that you and Mark don't believe you will ever be as "bad" as John, but is there truly a measuring stick for pain? We all experienced trauma, but my pain was different from yours, and yours was different from Mark's, and ours was different from John's.

Maybe we could make a deal. I'll continue to work on my baggage, and you could try to take some little steps with your own stuff. Nothing too heavy, but we can hope for an opening. One we can both walk through to create some room. A space where we can talk about the hard and difficult stuff without getting angry and disrespectful.

I don't want this letter to be the end. I refuse to believe that we'll never be able to share another laugh; a cherished memory; a time when life is beautiful, easy, and calm; a time when we are free from our collective anger and pain.

It's there for us. We just need to believe.

I love you.

CHAPTER 9
RED SEAL

THE SETTLEMENT OF DEADWOOD was illegal, built on Indian lands not yet surrendered. It was hastily pieced together by the rush of prospectors, and those who'd profit off their presence, during the gold rush of 1876. Squatter prospectors lived in tents and shanties and dug holes everywhere, looking for gold. Some likened the look of Deadwood to a prairie dog town.

The Sioux defended their territory, and shortly after the war of Little Big Horn and the death of Custer, they relinquished the Black Hills. By the time Deadwood was "officially" open for business, it was already the commercial centre for the raging gold rush fever of the Black Hills. It had in excess of two hundred stores, a postal service, a stagecoach, the telegraph, two sawmills, three banks, thirty hotels and eating houses, seventy saloons and dance halls, two daily newspapers, an academy, a church, and twenty lawyers.

In its heyday, Deadwood became known as the "wickedest camp on earth." It got its reputation because of establishments like the Gem Variety Theater, which opened in May 1876 and offered bawdy stage shows, drinking, gambling, dancing, and prostitution. It proved to be a gold mine in itself.

The town also became known for its lawlessness, and it was said that at night the town's citizens would hole up in their homes on the hillside while all the ruffians below them in the Badlands would kill each other off in drunken disputes settled with guns or knives.

Calamity Jane and Wild Bill Hickok were two of the larger-than-life Old West characters who were attracted to the area. I walked by a sign that declared it was the site of the No.10 Saloon where Wild Bill was shot in the back of the head by Jack McCall. Wild Bill had arrived in June and was shot dead on August 2.

McCall had felt insulted by Wild Bill the day before when he had lost several hands in a card game. Wild Bill gave him money for breakfast and suggested he not play again until he could cover his losses. The next day, drunk and resentful, McCall shot him from behind. A miner's court found him not guilty because he claimed Wild Bill had killed his brother. He later bragged that he had killed him in a fair gunfight. McCall would eventually hang for Wild Bill's murder after a second trial.

In 1961 the entire town of Deadwood was designated a national historic landmark for its well-preserved frontier architecture. The gold rush may have made the town, but the abandonment of the railroad; the bypass of Interstate 90; a mid-century decline in population; and major fires in 1959, 1982, and 1987 drove it into a disastrous state.

Ironically it was a return to its gambling roots that saved the town. Gaming was legalized in 1989, and receipts from its first years were much higher than expected. This enabled the Deadwood Historic Preservation Commission to accelerate several restoration projects, bringing vibrancy back to its architecture and attracting tourists.

I entered one of many gift stores and stood in front of a wall displaying Calamity Jane t-shirts. The one I was considering had Jane standing, holding her rifle, wearing a hat and a leather fringed jacket and pants. A gun belt with cartridges circles her waist. I don't know why, but she seems heftier or thicker than I imagined. *You know why. You've bought into the image that sells Calamity Jane, not the woman herself. Damn.*

To the right of her picture was the slogan *The bigger a man's gun the smaller his doodlewick.* Another t-shirt showed Jane leaning on her rifle: *Thought about being a lady, but then they told me I couldn't cuss.*

I was unable to decide on a favourite, so I bought neither. When I read about Calamity Jane later, I felt a kinship with her. Jane was known for her habit of wearing men's attire. Her father had a gambling problem, and her mother worked as a prostitute. When her father died, she took care of her five younger siblings by working as a dishwasher, a cook, a dance hall girl, and a prostitute.

Jane also suffered from depression, and she was an alcoholic who enlarged her own legend and fame using grandiose tales that were mostly proven to be false. I got her, sad, alone among men wanting to be as large and as popular as they were. And she succeeded if you measured in t-shirts.

I never did sex work, but I could easily imagine what it might have taken her to get there, and her grand telling of tales sounded like my behaviour at the height of my drunkenness. My grandiosity wasn't captured by a nation like hers was, but my need to be the centre of attention when drunk was much like what I remembered my mom Bev doing. The ring of her loud laughter while telling stories and flirting with those who'd pay attention to her.

What would Jane say today, knowing how difficult it still was for women if they dared to step into those spaces dominated by men? How would she feel, a century later, knowing the power structures were still held in the hands of men while women were endlessly fighting to access fair and equal opportunities? I suppose pulling a gun from her holster to let off a few rounds to express her displeasure, like she might have in the late 1800s, would be wrong? Maybe we should tell the others?

* * *

I'd like to say I hammered and beat down doors in a feminist struggle to find employment in a shop dominated by males, but I didn't. Instead, I got a lead from a friend who had heard that McNeil Motors, a General Motors dealership in Manotick, was looking for garage help. I knocked politely and told them I'd work hard, and they gave me a job. A few weeks later, I learned they hired me under a government incentive program to promote the entry of women into non-traditional occupations. A nod to the movement here, even though I was completely unaware of the second wave of feminism at the time, I had heard about bras being burned by angry, hairy, out-of-control women.

It was 1981, and the dealership paid me one dollar out of the five bucks I made per hour. The government paid the rest. I was worth the dollar an hour to McNeil, even though I was a woman, and even if all I ever did was take coffee orders, sweep the floor, clean the storage rooms, and hustle parts for the journeymen. I appreciated their dollar because I was being paid to work in a shop for the first time in my life. It made me feel strong, capable, and valued. A shout out honouring suffragettes and gospel socialism.

The auto body shop was much like other workshops. It felt cavernous, had large garage doors that could accept trucks, and was made of concrete block walls. Ducting and fans hovered from the ceiling, and airlines snaked along the walls. Time was marked by the sound of pistons thumping in an air compressor and the hiss of air it made when kicking off. Unlike machine shops (which smell of coolant and oils used for lubrication) and mechanic shops (which smell much the same—just throw in a little exhaust), body shops off-gas continuously from the chemicals in the products used to fix cars: fillers, fibreglass, resins, hardeners, activators, surfacers, putties, primers, etchers, strippers, thinners, reducers, paint, urethanes, and cleaners. It was not an environment for the sensitive.

The body shop's other constant occupant was sanding dust. It laid everywhere, like flour that was shaken over the counter before kneading bread. Dust was toxic to the process of painting, but it was unavoidable. My first chores in the shop consisted mostly of cleaning.

Before painting a vehicle, I'd prepare the paint booth. The booth was a hefty version of a large single-car garage. It was made of large steel sections bolted together. Inset fluorescent lights were lined up in rows on the ceiling and along the walls. It had barn doors with seals similar to those used on shipping containers. Cut-outs in the doors accepted filters like the polyester ones used for household furnaces. They had a sticky coating on the outer layer to catch fine dust particles. Huge exhaust fans on the roof pulled air through the front door filters, across the booth, and out exhaust vents in the back corners. The exhaust vents had filters made of layers of heavy paper cut in slits to allow the air to pass through them. They caught dust and overspray from the painting process.

The fans would be turned on, and I used compressed air to blow all the surfaces from front to back, following the airflow and changing the filters if needed. I'd then sweep the floor and spray it down with water. Afterwards, the painter would bring in the car and close the doors. The car would be washed down with a pre-cleaner before using a tack cloth to lightly wipe every surface, including the taped and papered sections. Lastly, I'd wet the floor down a second time before the painting started, careful not to splash any water onto the car.

Those first weeks I happily swept and cleaned and organized supplies. But I was also hazed by my co-workers. One morning I came in to find my coveralls tied up in almost undoable knots. Another day it was my bootlaces. Once I answered a call in the office, only to find that the phone had been covered in grease.

During the second week, Rob, the shop foreman, gave me a Styrofoam cup and told me to get a cup of paint thinner from the parts department. Eagerly I took the cup and walked quickly through the adjoining mechanic shop to where the parts counter was. The detailer in a corner bay, a big guy named Mike who wore his belt buckle on his hip so he wouldn't scratch the cars, turned away from me, but not before I saw him start laughing. I continued through the shop. Dale, a mechanic who specialized in electrical, worked in the second bay. When I passed by, he grinned, nodded, and wiped his hands on a shop rag. I put the cup down on the stainless-steel counter and asked Stan, the parts manager, for some paint thinner. He was an older guy with over-combed white hair, and he always wore blue work pants with a matching blue jacket. Expressionless, he said, "It'll just take me a sec." He disappeared into rows of shelving and came back with a gallon of thinner. He filled up the cup quickly and said, "Hurry it back."

I had gone about three car lengths before the bottom of the cup melted away, spilling thinner onto my boots and the floor. *Oh shit. Oh no!* I stood in astonishment, turning the cup over and around, and looking at the floor. Not wanting to get into trouble because I had "spilled" the thinner, I went back to Stan, showed him the cup, and asked if he had another one. "Nope, sorry." I was so concerned that I was oblivious to the mechanics, parts guys, and even the salesman taking an interest in my dilemma. I went back to the office and sheepishly asked Rob for another cup.

"I don't know what happened. It just melted."

He solemnly, and without comment, gave me another one, and back I went to parts and went through the same routine with Stan. This time, when it melted through, I looked up and saw the mechanics laughing. I had to laugh back.

Carl, the body man and Reese, the painter, ragged on me for days for not getting it the first time. I was a two-cupper. They obviously didn't know about my need to please and be obedient, the bastards.

After a few months of working as a helper, I asked to be signed up as an auto body repair apprentice. It would eventually mean more money with a graduated pay system, and I'd receive a commitment from the dealership for eight thousand hours of on-the-job training. It also meant I had to go to school for basic and advanced training courses at the local college. I was secretly ecstatic when the foreman agreed and called the local training office to start the paperwork. It was a big opportunity for me, and it would change my life.

I bought a used bench-top toolbox and started buying tools—like air sanders and board files, as well as socket and wrench sets—to fill it up. It was convenient to purchase tools and pay for them over a month or two, as both Snap-on and Mac Tools had trucks visit once a week.

In the early days, I didn't need many tools to strip cars of the parts to be taken off before prepping and painting them. The work meant a lot of sanding, and it was dusty and dirty, but I loved it. Unlike mechanical work, autobody repair and refinishing required an artistic hand and feel. I was taught to feel the surface I was preparing to seek out imperfections. My hands, not my eyes, would tell me if the substrate was ready or if it needed more attention. Not everyone had the talent or patience for the job. It was one of the reasons a lot of auto body helpers and apprentices come and go. Often, they showed up having done some weekend work or wanting to do some labour on their own car, and when they realized how much effort and skill it took to do the job, they disappeared.

It may also be that the trade was an inglorious one. It was a hard job, one made tougher if you were an apprentice. Only co-op students were lower on the shop ladder than the apprentice, and then there were some people—not just in auto body, but in all the trades—who thought that apprentices were good for cheap labour and that they could be treated badly. I was.

During one week, I spent days working on my hands and knees, cleaning out anchoring grooves in the shop floor for the frame straightening equipment. It was a shitty task, but as an apprentice, it was part of my job. My initial "fuck you" response was tempered by the understanding that I was told to do the job because I was an apprentice, not because I was a woman. But this was also the time, when I was on my hands and knees, when the parts manager sexually harassed me. Stan stood over my head and said, "Just where a woman should be, on her knees," while he pulled at his zipper.

In 1982 I went to Algonquin College for my basic training. Trade school lasted eight weeks, and I was "paid" by unemployment insurance. I drove a motorcycle, and I was slim and muscular from working at a physical job. Dressed in my work clothes, I looked like a boy. My classmates and teachers assumed that I was just another guy.

Most of the shops at Algonquin College were in Block A, and the main hallway was called Vulture's Alley. Women who ventured down the hall were subjected to catcalls, invitations to engage in sex, and rough commentary about their bodies. It was rare to see a woman alone.

In the '80s, smoking was still allowed in the school, so during break time, the benches lining the hall were taken up with men, some smoking, most drinking coffee, all talking tech or gossiping. I'd sit outside the body shop door, my hands dirty—I was afraid to go into the cleanup room off the shop floor because I thought it might have urinals in it.

Steve sat with me, and he'd elbow my arm when women would walk towards us. "Hey man, look at those tits." And "look at that ass. Tight, eh?" when they'd pass. I'd grunt and look away, my face hot. It was more than awkward. I was afraid to tell him I was a woman. I was ashamed I was one because I didn't want to get rejected.

After a week, I stayed late and tried to tell Mr. Smith, my teacher. Words completely escaped me. I stuttered and stalled and mumbled a few words about how much noise my mother's bra made in the dryer because of its underwire, before blurting loudly, "If I was as well-endowed as my mother, there wouldn't be a problem." The next day he called the class together in the shop and said that he was "proud to introduce the first woman enrolled in the Auto Body Program at Algonquin College." It was a surprise to everybody, apparently, except Steve. "I knew it," he said. "I looked down your shirt."

He wouldn't have seen a bra because I never wore one after the last bra my mom bought for me shredded itself from wear. Going braless wasn't a statement about the feminist alliance or a fist pump for the sisters—it was just a matter of being too embarrassed to go buy one. I've never owned a real bra since, but I've come to wear a sports bra—using the formula of mass plus gravity times decades just means a little extra shifting and lifting to have my nipples pointed in the right direction, but it worked.

Some things changed after I was outed as a woman. I used the cleanup room because I found out there were no urinals, only a half-moon washbasin and some lockers. My work got a lot more attention. This scrutiny petered out when the guys saw I could do the work quicker and better than they could. A few celebrated my abilities, but most of them muted my skills, ignoring me.

The ongoing harassment of women in Vulture's Alley didn't change. In some instances, it was ramped up when I was around. I think they were testing me to see if I had any objection. I didn't. I wondered why women would walk down the hall at all because they didn't have any classes in A Block. I wanted to tell them there were other safer ways to get to the mall beside the college. At the time, I wanted to be more boy than girl, but I didn't think membership required me to taunt the women either. After all, there were several men who didn't engage, who seemed embarrassed by the vulgar displays.

I was also very tight-lipped about being gay and thought if I made any disparaging remarks about women to gain kinship with my comrades, then I'd be labelled a dyke or butch. Dykes and butches weren't part of their class either.

After school, I went back to McNeil Motors and worked for another year before being lured away by the offer of a couple more dollars an hour. It was common in auto body and the other trades for employers to poach employees who had already been trained. It didn't work out, and I bounced around a few more shops before returning to McNeil to finish my apprenticeship. I was grateful they took me back.

By that time in my apprenticeship, I had graduated to doing mostly metalwork: fabricating panels for rust repair, collision repairs, and major panel replacement; minor frame realignment; and prepping and painting cars if needed.

There was one memorable moment during my second stint at McNeil Motors. It was a summer day, and I'd pulled a vehicle outside to let the sun accelerate the drying time of some primer I'd sprayed on the lower section of the rear quarter panel. I sanded the primer outside, and because it was on the lower section, I had to crouch.

During one crouch, I felt a tickle on my lower leg above my work boots. I stood up and shook my leg. All good. I crouched up and down several times to give my knees a break. The day was hot. I felt the tickle again, and again shook my leg.

On my last crouch, I noticed a large lump, about the size of a flattened golf ball, on my thigh underneath my coveralls. I jumped up and screamed and then started running towards the open garage doors of the shop.

In my peripheral vision, I could see the surprised expressions of the guys in the shop as they stopped their work to watch me sprint from the parking lot. I'm not a runner, but I made pretty good time.

I dashed into the paint booth. By now, my screams had settled into short frantic gasps: "Omigod, omigod, omigod." I hopped from one foot to the other. It was fruitless, especially being in a hurry, to get coveralls off over work boots, and trying to untie boots when in distress is fucking impossible. It was like fumbling keys to the getaway car in some horror movie when the bad guy was coming for you.

My fingers were like stubs, unable to find any purchase. Still hopping, I took a razor blade out of my pocket—I used them for trimming tape—and cut the laces where they wound around the top of my right boot. I pulled the laces and threw the boot, hitting the wall of the paint booth, shaking the metal panels.

I bounced on my sock foot, ripped my left boot off in the same manner and flung it out the booth door, where it skidded along the concrete floor, clearing dust in its wake. I was still hopping and circling erratically and gasping the only word I was able to get out, "omigod."

Managing to unbutton my coveralls, I pushed them down and pulled them off by standing on the cuffs. One sock went with one leg. I straightened up and backed away from the carnage, breathless and naked, but for one sock and my underwear, looking at the biggest beetle I'd ever seen, a giant water bug.

I did the heeby jeeby dance, rubbing my hands along my legs, arms, and body, checking them—for what, I wasn't sure. Maybe baby beetles? When I was satisfied, I circled slowly with my arms up, hands on my head, my breathing slowing with my heart rate.

With eyes on the beetle, I collected my boots and redressed. Using a broom, I corralled it into a dustpan and delivered it outside, where I gently flung it into the closest ditch.

My intimacy with the beetle was great fodder for coffee break conversations when I went back to finish my advanced training at Algonquin. It was possible that I even outdid Calamity Jane with my dramatic re-telling of it. I'd like to think she would have been proud, maybe enough to call me friend.

Nothing much had changed at the College since my basic training. While Vulture's Alley was still treacherous for women, there were more tradeswomen—an electrician and a couple of carpenters—who belonged in the hallway. We barely acknowledged each other, preferring to stand alone, tough as the men we worked with. I was as indifferent to them as they were to me, and we radiated an aggressive competition in those shop hallways even though we were in different trades.

Affirmative action may have opened the doors to male-dominated blue-collar workplaces, but the movement stopped there. A feminist perspective did not inform any of the workshops I spent time in. They were male-dominated, and their motto was *Put up and shut up or get out*. These inner sanctums were rough and tough places to work. It was about survival, and it was almost impossible for women to thrive because of the many barriers they faced: sexual harassment, bullying, abuse, lower pay, and paternalistic and hierarchal structures. There were no washrooms or personal spaces for women, and the only personal protective equipment available, like coveralls and gloves, was designed and made for men.

For some women, these barriers were enough to drive them away; others left because of the constant subtle hum, a simmering undercurrent that they didn't belong. The energy always came from someone—the clerk at the parts counter, the supervisor, your workmates, or the secretary in the office. The judgment was suffocating and defeating if you succumbed.

By this time, the second wave of feminist action was petering out. Its consciousness was disappearing into bureaucratization and academia. It had been absorbed by countless activist groups and grassroots movements driven by the feminist perspective. Feminism didn't disappear—it just looked different.

There was some initial activism and recognition for women in trades at the college, but the program was understaffed and marginalized. Competing for funds with "real" trades programming meant its existence would be a future footnote.

I graduated from the auto body program at Algonquin College with the highest marks the program had ever seen. In '85, after I finished my apprenticeship at McNeil Motors, I wrote my provincial exam and received my trade licence as an Auto Body and Collision Damage Repairer. My exam marks were above the benchmark for excellence, so I was awarded a Red Seal Inter-Provincial Certificate. The Red Seal standard is a huge achievement for apprentices. It provides you with membership in an exclusive group of tradespeople, and the certification removes obstacles to employment in other provinces. It gave me a lot of pride to say I had a Red Seal.

I would like to say that with my new qualifications, clutched in a fist held high, I kicked down the garage door at the Municipal Garage Complex of the City of Ottawa, but I can't. I had heard from a friend the garage's driver was moving to a new position chauffeuring the mayor, and there was a vacancy. I got the position. The big shop boss never called me Lorrie; instead, he called me Lenny, the name of the driver I replaced.

There was no question that most people who worked at the complex were backward or stalled in their thinking about women working in the trades. There were women onsite as office staff, but I was the only woman who worked in the shops at the time. The garage was hostile and intimidating but also welcoming and friendly. Some of the women operators wouldn't wait for equipment repairs in the garage, they stood outside, while others bounced right in and ragged the men as much as they were ragged by them.

While both were ways women managed, the garage environment was toxic to humans. Men, insecure and fearful for reasons known only to them, acted out aggressively, feeding the wolf pack and not wanting to be shunned by their peers.

A favourite was pinching the balls of their co-workers. There was also lots of wrestling and horseplay. Once a welder went through a shop door window, seriously injuring his arm. Then there was the time a co-op student was stuck up in a loader bucket, where he was sprayed with water in front of an audience. Others would verbally abuse a target all day long, and then they'd walk out together joking and laughing after they punched out for the day. Not each other but the time clock.

The garage complex was like a men's sports team locker room, and it had all the locker room issues—intimidation, hazing, aggression, bullying, and superiority—all tainted with a need to be the winner, whatever the cost. I wasn't suggesting that all men in the garage were players, but the majority were. And then there were the players on the bench. They may not have been full participants in every game, but their silence condoned the aggressiveness and condemned the targets.

Every day women had to walk into this toxic work environment. We were ill-prepared for it. I grew up with brothers and knew how to fight and scrap for leftovers but navigating through a shop populated with testosterone-fuelled men out to prove their daily worth was scary. The men who worked at the city garage weren't the same as the boys I had hung out with during my machine shop course or the countrified mechanics at McNeil Motors. This was the big league, and—like I had done with my brothers—I took it on with bravado and above-average work and effort. I gave as good as I got. I counted myself fortunate; it was hard to imagine how it was for women who didn't have any previous shop experience, or brothers to fight with, or who wanted to act like men to belong. I saw it as equal opportunity in name only. They opened the door, threw us in, and slammed it shut. No one was prepared.

I worked for the City of Ottawa for almost four years, most of that time in the auto body shop. I loved the work—replacing front ends on police cars, fabricating step sides for ladder trucks, welding quarter panels, and painting work vans the city's signature bright orange colour. Rumour had it that a previous mayor had chosen the colour to make the vehicles as visible as possible, an attempt to discourage workers from slinking around and slacking off.

I found the work empowering. There was nothing like backing up an engine ladder truck successfully into a bay to make you feel on top of the world, especially if you had a critical audience. I also loved the position, the idea of being able to say I worked in the city garage. I appreciated the pay and liked most of the men who worked there. I bought into the machismo attitude of the garage, and my co-workers took care of me in return.

A few years in, my teacher from trade school contacted me about a job opening teaching shop. The Office of Equal Opportunity lobbied my supervisor to support my request for a leave of absence from the city to teach at Algonquin College. It was granted. Would the men I worked with have been given the same support?

By the time I left the city to work full time at Algonquin College, it had been almost ten years since I knocked on the dealership door at McNeil Motors. I had no idea then that I'd be offered an apprenticeship opportunity and how it would come to change my life. I was about to become a teacher, an unfathomable thought I'd never entertained. It was the feminist movement, with its demands for equal opportunities, that forced the door off its hinges for me. I just didn't know it at the time.

CHAPTER 10
HORSES IN THE SAND

I HEADED SOUTH FROM DEADWOOD on Highway 385 and stopped to have dinner at the Pactola Visitor Center in the Black Hills National Forest.

I pulled up to the beach area and unloaded my cooler. Skinny Bitch, a shame and guilt expert, laid out cottage cheese, tuna, avocado, cherry tomatoes, and a mixed salad. Skinny Bitch's sister, Fat Chick, had been dormant on the trip except for the time she made an appearance at Bear's Paw Bakery in Jasper. When I was in line for a coffee, she kept poking me to look at a ceramic jar on a shelf. Written on its side in block letters was *COME TO THE DARK SIDE. WE HAVE COOKIES.* Skinny showed up, and we all argued back and forth, irritating each other in line until I got to the counter. We compromised on a berry muffin.

I assembled my salad at a picnic table on the beach and sat down facing the reservoir. The sun was setting on three kids and a black lab playing in the water. From their shouts and laughter, I learned the dog's name was Bella. She came over to greet me with her tail wagging. She reminded me of Rafter, our very lovable black lab, who Paula and I euthanized right before my trip. That dog followed me everywhere. Whether I was in the house or out on the land, she was there. When I'd put her in the back of the Edge for a drive, she always jumped over into the back seat and sat with her front paws on the floor so she could lay her head on the centre console. I would reach back to pet her head, and her tail thumped the seat repeatedly.

Bella was a little taller and leaner than Rafter, but she had the same sweet disposition. Her tail frantically wagged back and forth, and her hips wiggled in time with its movement. I rubbed her ears and held her head in my hands to look in her eyes before she ran back to the water.

An older, mustachioed maintenance man wearing a ball cap and a light tan work shirt with a park maintenance logo on it walked the beach area in a grid pattern, picking up garbage along the beach. When he came close, I asked, "Is the gate gonna close soon?"

"No. You can stay here all night if you'd like," he replied without losing a step in his grid walk. I overheard him talking with the woman whose kids were still in the water. They talked camping and touched on the fact that the concession people have all pulled out: "It's the end of season, and Loop A is still open for camping."

When he made his way back, I asked him about camping. He told me that I could camp for free. There was no one around to collect the fees, and the lower women's washroom in Loop A was the only one open. He said there were lots of waterspouts available and that there should be enough firewood down there to have a fire. "Camp there until the Forest Service comes and tells you can't," he encouraged.

I thanked him and told him I'd go over and check it out. I finished my dinner and packed up the cooler. It was funny how Skinny Bitch and Fat Chick always managed to skip out on the cleaning up part.

He continued picking trash and then came back over to me. "Don't you want to know how to get there?"

"Sure."

"Up there," he said, pointing towards his left. "Turn right after about three-eighths of a mile, go past a cove with boats, and then turn right again. Then take your next left, go past the hut—don't worry about it, no one will be there—go to where the garbage bins are and turn right past them."

"So, right, right, left, and then right. Is that right?"

He chuckled. "I figure it is."

I was closing my door when he returned again to give me directions to the gas stations that had laundry facilities, gas, and ice because "it's good to know where those things are."

I circled through Loop A and was blessed with a site overlooking the reservoir, Pactola Lake. At an uphill campsite was a Ford Transit with a Vermont licence plate. The couple who emerged were older, lean, and fit. There were two road bikes strapped to a carrier on the back of the van.

Down the hill to the south, at the next site over, were a young couple in their twenties. They had a truck, a boat trailer, and an old canvas tent, the style that used exterior galvanized poles to hold it up. They were enjoying a large fire.

I dressed in warm clothes, started a small fire of my own from scraps of wood that I quickly and easily scavenged from a couple of firepits, and used my headlamp to read a mystery novel I had been meaning to finish. I took the novel to bed around midnight and read until I fell asleep.

It had become a pattern, and not just on the road, that I woke up after three to four hours of sleep. That morning I woke up at four-thirty. My mind was circling and looping, full of questions. *Where am I going? What should I do? Why am I feeling the need to be on the move? Should I go home? What's Paula doing? Should I call her again or wait for her to call me?*

I read some more and then floated in and out of sleep until six-thirty, when a beautiful sun rose out the back window of the Ford. It was an exceptional sunrise, like a lot that I had witnessed—like a lot we had all witnessed, I suppose—but it didn't meet the gold standard of the sun setting or rising on the prairies.

I thought I had experienced the most beautiful sunsets over the granite outcroppings and woods of the boreal forest, but my bragging rights were smashed when I saw my first prairie sunset driving west towards Saskatoon. I was awed, and it stirred a deep appreciation of the poems and prose that had been written in an attempt to fully capture the essence of the enduring prairie sun, as elusive as the spirit of the soul.

I hoped the rising sun would bring some needed warmth for the day. It had been a cold night, and I was very happy with my new blanket. I reluctantly got out of bed, layered on clothes, slid out of the Edge and into my boots, put on a jacket, and made some coffee with a percolator on my Coleman stove.

I noticed the young man running to his truck for wood. He used lighter fluid to get a fire going. His partner came out of the canvas tent, and they headed down to the shore along a dirt track, carved out of the ground like a snake winding around rocks and trees.

It wasn't long before I heard a motor start and saw them in their boat heading towards the middle of the lake. He was in shorts and a t-shirt, and she didn't seem to have much more on herself. They were back within fifteen minutes. I saw her huddled up in the front, and he wasn't sitting as tall as when they first left.

I finished my mug of coffee, putting the rest from the percolator in a thermos. The biker couple from Vermont were up and dressed in their bike shorts and tops. The young couple, buried in clothes, unhitched the boat trailer, got in the truck, and left. I suspected they might have thought catching and cooking their own breakfast would be kind of romantic, but a hot breakfast in town was a warmer alternative to spending time half-naked in the middle of the lake on a cold morning.

The young man kicked out their fire before they left, and plumes of smoke drifted through my site. I closed the doors to the Ford so my clothes and bedding wouldn't absorb the smoke—a nod to Paula. She wouldn't complain, but she always asked me to store the jacket I'd wear, either when keeping the fire for ceremony or burning brush, in the garage and not with her coats in the closet.

During my drive out of the reservoir, I pulled over to where some slate-like stone was exposed. It was the Sioux who called the area *Paha Sapa*, meaning "hills that are black." The layers of stone were dark grey, and the ponderosa pines looked like they had been touched with charcoal along their bark edges and limb knots. The hills were also known to the Sioux as *Wamakoagnaka E'cante*, or "the heart of everything that is."

I picked up a piece of stone and laid a pinch of tobacco down in its place before getting back into the Edge. I was taught by an Elder that when you take something from Mother Earth, you should offer tobacco in return because "tobacco medicine teaches us about reciprocity."

I stopped at the Hill City Café. Fat Chick was tired because she hadn't slept well for a few days, and she was salivating over the potatoes, sausages, and bacon. Skinny quickly ordered what had lately become my usual breakfast: two eggs over easy, with wheat toast and sliced tomatoes. I imagined the tomatoes as potatoes, cut up and fried with onions and enough butter to make them crispy and tender.

When I got to the cash, Chick stared at the biggest cinnamon rolls she'd ever seen; they were as wide as a cantaloupe and as high as a short mug of coffee. Some had white icing, and others had melted sugar. I leaned into the counter. They smelled deliciously of bread, yeast, caramel, sugar, butter, and spice. She wanted to roll in them, to lather her breasts and belly in icing and soft yummy bits of dough. I yanked her out the door.

* * *

I sat cross-legged in the middle of a worn carpet. The rug—like the chair and the couch pushed against the concrete wall of the basement— used to be in the living room, but it had been rolled up and shoved down the stairs by Mom during a spring cleanup. It was one of her crazy phases where she emptied the living room of its couch, chairs, drapes, books, and plants to clean and then rearrange the furniture. I remember how sore and tired my arms were from stripping the old wax off the hardwood floors. I had spent most of one day on my knees, inhaling the harsh sting of solvents and using rags and brushes to work the dull and dirty wax out of the corners. I really wanted to use the electric polisher to shine the floors before the new rug was laid down, but John claimed that chore first.

Sunlight from the window high in the corner shined on the open pages of a hardcover book sitting in my lap. Dust motes danced and floated in the light as I turned the pages slowly and carefully. It was difficult to grab the corners because my nails were bitten short and bloody. My hands, like the rest of me, were dirty from playing in the bush and squatting alongside the road. I used a twig to draw horses in the sand that had been pulled from the gravel during a recent storm.

The vibrant hand-drawn pictures on the pages kept my attention, and when I touched them, I felt good and safe. There were also many words, but they hadn't become my friends like the colourful pictures had.

I knew I was supposed to be upstairs washing my hands so I could set the coffee table for his dinner. I hoped they would forget about me. It wouldn't be the first time I had slipped their mind until they suddenly remembered they needed a drink made, or a cold beer pulled from the fridge, or the channel changed on the television.

    I pulled a rock from the front pocket of my shorts. It took a long time after school, kicking through the gravel beside the highway, to find the perfect one. It was slightly bowl-shaped, fitting nicely in my palm. It should work to hold the top of the fire bow I wanted to make. The boys in my class at school told me that being able to start a fire to stay warm and cook food when you are alone in the forest was really important.

    I rubbed the rough surface and imagined sitting beside my fire; I could see it flickering and dancing just like the ones we always had when we went camping at Driftwood. I saw my fire in the middle of a clearing. A wigwam sat to the side. It was in a place where I could run and play and be free.

    I tucked the rock back into my pocket, deciding I would hide it when I went upstairs, in the back of the top drawer of my dresser with the rope for the bow. I sawed the piece of rope off a spool I had found stuffed under his workbench.

    I was still not sure where I would get a knife to carve the notches that held the rope in the wood. I lifted one yesterday from the kitchen after breakfast, but it was dull and kept slipping off the small, curved piece of wood I had picked for the bow. I decided to try the small axe that he kept in the back shed. How could I sneak it out?

    Footsteps stomped across the ceiling, and I looked up, waiting for Mom to open the door and call out again for me. I had snuck downstairs to the basement after the first time she yelled for me to come home so I could look through my book. I laid my belly down on the old carpet and swiped my arm back and forth under the couch until I felt the pillowcase I'd stuffed the book into. At first, I was scared because I couldn't feel it and thought one of my brothers had gotten to it, like the time they'd found the pictures I'd coloured and waved them at me so I would chase them. I tried not to cry too hard when I got the pictures back ripped and wrinkled.

    I heard Mom walking back to the couch, and I returned to the book. I rubbed the page showing how to make moccasins. My dirty fingers left marks. When I had seen the pictures the first time, I pleaded with Mom to buy some leather so I could try and make my own. She laughed drunkenly and slurred out a no. Even though I knew better, I kept asking, getting louder and pushier. She got red-faced and angry, and I thought I might get the paddle, but instead, she yelled at me to get out. I went into the bush behind the neighbour's house and climbed a tree to watch the traffic speeding along the highway.

Mom wasn't always drunk. Last summer, she let me make a leather wallet. I'd seen the project on a poster taped to the front door of the bowling alley and ran home right away to ask for the money. On the day of the activity, I woke up early in the morning, but it took forever for the afternoon to come so I could run down to the town centre. I remember opening the bag the kit came in, smelling the leather, and feeling the stamped pictures on the outer panel. I was so focused on following the instructions and lacing the wallet together that I never really heard the repeated suggestions from the woman running the program that I should make a change purse instead.

I turned the page and then the next, and the next, passing over beadwork designs and thunderbird symbols. I stopped at the eagle dance costume. A man with an eagle head hat held out his arms, covered in layers of black and white feathers crossing over his shoulders. It made me wonder what it would be like to fly. I imagined seeing the ground from above and wondered if I could ever run fast enough to take off. I didn't think I'd be able to, and where would I even find feathers? And if I did, where would I hide them?

I lifted the back cover, and the book fell open to the teepee pages. I had folded the corner of the page to keep my place. I smoothed it out and hoped the librarian wouldn't notice. The card in the envelope glued to the back cover said I took it out six times in a row. I had to return it the following week on Wednesday.

I touched the picture of a young woman inside the teepee. She was sitting beside a fire, lifting the lid from a pot, and there were some sticks for the fire beside her. I closed my eyes and promised to build my own place far in the bush. A place that would have more than what my tree fort had now—it would have a roof that didn't leak, proper windows instead of car door glass, and it would be my very own. I wouldn't cry or be afraid when I was there, and I'd only invite nice people to come. And those who wouldn't yell at me.

"Lorrie," shouted my mom. I hadn't heard her tromp across the floor to the door. I closed the book, wrapped it back up in the pillowcase

I had taken from the linen closet upstairs, and slid it back under the couch out of sight.

"Yeah?" I yelled back.

"What're you doing down there? I've been calling and calling," she complained.

"Nothing," I said.

"Well, get up here. Your father is going to be home soon, and I need the table set."

He got off the bus at five minutes to five o'clock every day. It was less than a minute from the bus stop to our house. That day he looked like he was already in a bad mood when he sat down heavily with a grunt on the couch. My stomach started to feel sour. I went into the kitchen, where my mom shoved his dinner plate at me. "Take that out to your father."

I sat his dinner down on a placemat between the utensils I laid out a few minutes earlier. He picked up his newspaper. "Get me a beer." I always made sure the paper was where it was supposed to be every night when he got home: on the coffee table to the left of his setting. Returning to the kitchen, I looked back to see his reaction. *Will he know I opened it?* Even Mom wasn't allowed to open or read the newspaper until he finished. I carefully realigned the creases and edges, smoothing it out when I positioned it. He didn't seem to notice.

He took the bottle and held it up to see the level. "Did you take a sip?" he asked me accusingly.

"No, no, I didn't. I promise," I whined.

"Are you sure?" He sneered. The look on his face said he wanted to hit something. I pushed my palms down on my shorts, wiping them dry, and shook my head. "No, I didn't. I promise."

After a moment, he grunted in acceptance, took a large swallow, and went back to his newspaper. I sagged. The last time I took a sip, it had been too much. He noticed right away and slapped my head hard when I bent over to put the bottle down. My ears were ringing, and my cheek felt hot, but I held my tears until he told me to go. My brothers and I knew not to run but to stand and wait until he was finished. It was always worse if he had to catch us.

Mom started yelling outside for the boys to come for dinner. The screen door slammed shut, and my three brothers rushed into the kitchen. We elbowed and pushed each other out of the way to get at the pots and pans on the stove. There were mashed potatoes, French green beans, and some partridge breasts taken out of the freezer and cooked in a chicken soup mix.

We took our plates to the dining room table to eat. Mom sat down with her meal on the opposite side of the curved couch that took up the back wall of the living room. I remembered earlier times when our loud laughter and boisterous play would get us into trouble at the table because our attention wasn't on our plates. Later it came from our pushing and complaining.

"Get your chair away from mine."

"Mom, tell Craig to stop taking my potatoes."

"Save some spaghetti for me."

"It's your turn for the dishes."

"I'm washing."

"No, it's my turn. I'm washing."

"You're stupid."

"Mom, John didn't save any spaghetti for me."

"You didn't catch me at tag."

"Yes, I did, you loser."

My brothers attacked their food like our dog Shep used to when I put down his bowl. He was always chained up to the fence in the backyard until one day he wasn't there anymore.

They dropped their dishes into the kitchen sink and ran out the door to finish delivering papers so they could go to their friends' places. It used to be that the slowest one had to do the dishes because they were last. Somehow, it had become my chore. My brothers laughed when I complained. "It's your job because you're a girl."

The partridge was dry and took forever to chew, but I ate the breast because he had shot the birds on a hunting trip. I shuffled my fork around the green beans, chewed some slivers and avoided the red things. I got up from the table and looked for some more potatoes, but my brothers had emptied the pot.

I scraped the beans off my plate into the garbage can under the sink and went into the living room, picking up their dirty dishes.

"What time are you going to be home tonight?" he asked Mom.

"Late. I need to cover Gary's shift."

That funny thing happened. My stomach twisted, and my breath snagged, making me cough. I got him another beer and filled the sink with warm water and soap.

Mom had pinned up her hair, darkened her eyebrows, and glued on some eyelashes. Red lipstick brightened her lips. She opened the corner cupboard in the kitchen and reached behind the box of powdered milk for a pack of Rothmans cigarettes. She slid the pack into her purse, smiled and winked at me. She hadn't quit smoking like she told him, and we all kept it a secret. We knew her hiding spots and often stole some. She couldn't tell him to punish us for it.

The water was cold, and there were no suds left when I dunked the last pot into the sink. I washed it anyway and dried it quickly with the tea towel. The towel was as damp as the pot. I thought I should get a dry one from the cupboard, but I didn't.

The television was turned off, and I heard the opening whistling wails of the soundtrack to the cowboy movie *The Good, the Bad and the Ugly*. I knew it because he told me I was the bad and the ugly. I went to the door and cautiously looked back. He was lying on the couch with an arm over his eyes. There was still some beer in his bottle.

I placed my foot carefully down on the part of the tread closest to the wall. And then the next, and the next. I opened the door and held it while it closed so it wouldn't slam.

I walked down the street, looking down at my canvas runners, and skipped over the cracks in the asphalt. I felt the weight of the stone bouncing in my pocket.

I knocked on the back door of Jane's house.

"Is Jane home?"

Jane's mom held the screen door open, looking down on me. The flowered apron she wore was wet and stained. I knew her look. Claire's mother had the same look. One day on our way to school, I had convinced Claire to take a shortcut, even though I knew it was longer and would make us late. On our way, I picked up a dead squirrel, and the teacher I tried to give it to insisted on calling the janitor and the principal and my mom and Claire's mom. I didn't understand the "stupid fucking mess" Mom said I'd made.

I looked down at my runners, wiggled my toes.

"Jane's doing her homework."

"Okay. Thanks, Mrs. Slater." I walked back down the driveway and went past the house on the corner where the lady had caught me one afternoon pulling out her plants and flowers. She was really nice and rubbed my shoulder when I started to cry. She asked me not to do it again, and she said that if I did, she'd tell my mom. I'm glad she didn't because Mom would have probably told him, like all the other times she had told on us. "Get upstairs and wait for your father." Waiting always meant getting the belt. When he was in a bad mood, he'd make us pull down our pants before bending over.

It was dark when I crawled into bed. I had run right upstairs after coming in from playing on the swings in the back bush. I pumped my legs and body hard back and forth. I got up high enough to get over the top bar before stalling and falling back. When I left, there was just enough light to see the bats flying through the clearing above the swings.

I heard Craig and Mark in their own room across the hall wrestling. John was complaining and yelling at them to stop. I stared at the closed door. He insisted on having the doors closed for bedtime. I laid rigid and straight, and my arms were outside the covers down by my sides. *Maybe I could try to hide in the closet. You're so stupid—he just saw you come in.* I thought again about hiding under the bed, this time closer to the wall. *Now you're really stupid—he knew you were there, and you crawled back out when he told you to, you loser.*

The television went quiet, and the stairs creaked with his weight. I heard him opening the door to the boys' room and telling Craig and Mark to get into their own beds and turn out the light.

He filled my room like a giant I once saw at the movies. The door closed behind him, and he hovered like a dark shadow. His breathing was hoarse and heavy. I smelled stale beer and his sweat. My heart started to punch against the covers tightened across my chest, my stomach twinged, and my hands coiled into fists. I closed my eyes and pretended he wasn't really real.

The floor moaned when he knelt beside the bed. He inhaled, taking the air away from me. A large hand reached under the covers, circled my leg, pulling me around. He pushed my legs open, grabbed my hips, and brought me towards his mouth. When I felt his beard and tongue, I left the room through the window and sat on a large pine tree branch in our front yard.

I woke up the next morning in a wet bed. *Now, you're in trouble. Ugly and Bad.* I pulled back the covers and stripped the sheets from the bed. The mattress was stained, but when it dried, it'd match all the other stains. He would have gone to work, but Mom would see me bringing the sheets downstairs, so I rolled them up with my underwear and hid them in the closet. I'd get to them after school.

"Did you make your bed?" Mom asked me tiredly. Her hair was lopsided, the blush on her cheeks was smeared, and there was some glue left on her eyelashes. She was smoking and drinking coffee. A clear glass sat empty beside an open packet of ENO.

"Yes," I said.

"Are you going to have some breakfast?"

"No, I have to go." I threaded a belt through the loops of my shorts.

"What are you doing with your brother's belt?"

"Nothing." I worked it out while pulling the sheets off the bed. I'd sneak the axe out of the back shed by hanging it through the belt and hiding it under my sweater until I could get it to the bush.

"Where are you going?"

"Nowhere."

* * *

The child in this story is my hero, and she is who I aspire to be today. I truly believe I am closer to the person I was born in this moment than at any other time in my life. It's been quite a walk.

Finding this little girl, who crouched beside the road to draw pictures of horses in the sand with a twig, has been a slow shedding of my conditioning and the societal expectations imposed on me at the hands of family, school, and society. It is ongoing, daily work.

I'm reminded of an Elder who told me that I carried everything I needed to live my best life possible. She also shared that I'm not broken, so there's no need for me to look for external fixes like losing weight, buying something new and shiny, or seeking out new relationships. I was whole and held it all.

This process of ridding myself of the harmful impositions as well as working within my childhood trauma has been an affirming journey of remembering, a recognition of my true self. I'm grateful for it every day.

CHAPTER 11
I KNOW NOTHING

THE MEMORIAL WASN'T AS I IMAGINED. I expected a large stone carving, a statue, magnificent but modest and humble. Maybe a plaque or two describing Crazy Horse's feats as a warrior, all placed quietly around a naturally landscaped clearing.

I was taken aback when I saw the colossal mountain carving. It was unlike anything I'd ever seen. I stood and stared at it from the parking lot. Crazy Horse, even in his unfinished state, was striking. The natural grey colour of the mountain had turned to hues of sand where the stone had been blasted and carved away to reveal his face. Also visible from a mile away was an etching of the profile of his horse. When finished, the mountain monument will show Crazy Horse sitting on his horse with his arm extended, pointing out over his ancestral lands. It is expected to be 641 feet long and 563 high, eclipsing the neighbouring presidents carved into Mount Rushmore.

Not only awed by the proportions, I was impressed by the vision, the engineering, and just the amount of plain hard work that it had taken so far for sculptor Ziolkowski and his family to "carve us a mountain so that the white man will know the Red man had great heroes also." The request was made of Ziolkowski in 1939 by Chief Henry Standing Bear.

I texted a picture to Paula.

Wow, that is crazy!

Okay? *Did she mean to be funny?* If I could have seen her face, I'd have my answer.

The carving of Thunder Mountain began in 1948. Pictures of its dedication ceremony showed Korczak Ziolkowski, Governor

Michelson, and David Humphreys Miller—an artist and specialist in the culture of the northern plains Indian—as well as Red Bear, Comes Again, High Eagle, Little Soldier, and Standing Bear. It was Miller who brought together these last survivors of the Battle of Little Bighorn for the dedication, and they were pictured standing in some photos and dancing in others. I wondered where the women were.

My wonder continued when I saw several prominent portraits in the Indian Museum. They were all men, high on the walls. Sitting below some of those pictures were women at stations throughout the museum complex, making and selling their crafts. Women were represented in a few of what looked like family photos and in some of the artefacts and clothing displayed on the walls and in glass cases.

The photo that struck me the most was of a gentrified Chief Standing Bear sitting in the centre with his wife Victoria and son Luther standing behind him. His two other sons, Henry and Willard, were sitting in the foreground. The men in the family were dressed in a domesticated style: suit jackets, shirts, and ties for the boys, and an ascot for Standing Bear. Victoria was wearing a black dress with a white high-necked collar and bib. Standing Bear and his wife had long hair, while their sons' locks were styled in a short fashion, with side parts. None were smiling, and they all had flat, uninspired expressions. The image is not dated, but I guessed it would have been taken in the early 1890s, before Chief Standing Bear died in 1898.

The black-and-white photo seemed out of place in the space, a large hall filled with energy emanating from the rich and vibrant colours of the Sioux Nation. It was like someone had taken their vitality and then propped the family up in a display devoid of colour that represented the dominant culture.

It was in opposition to this dominance of their lands, especially of the Black Hills, that some Lakota Sioux objected to the project. Women relatives of Crazy Horse expressed that their voices had been left out of the decision to have him memorialized. They believed it should have been a family decision, reached by consensus, rather than a sole independent petition of Ziolkowski by Standing Bear.

In the spirit of Crazy Horse's refusal to be photographed, there were Sioux activists, as well as medicine men and women, who felt the monument was not only a desecration of his memory, but also a scarring of the sacred Hills themselves. They saw it as hypocrisy, much like the stain of Mount Rushmore that had already been hacked out of their ancestral lands.

Then there were those in the larger community who challenged the many millions the Ziolkowskis have made off the privately funded project that had been under construction for over seventy years. The family ran several privately owned businesses on the land and paid royalties to the Crazy Horse Memorial Foundation.

I was left conflicted. While the mountain carving is an epic human feat I could admire, I agreed with those who opposed it. It was a corruption of sacred lands. I was glad I took the time, though, because I was better for experiencing a small sense of the living history of the Sioux Nation.

And I felt privileged to have met Lula Red Cloud, a Grandmother and direct descendent of Chief Red Cloud, war chief and leader of the Oglala Sioux. Before I left the memorial, I stopped at her workbench.

She sat quietly while I browsed her work. Towels made thick by wadding were wrapped around each side of the curved back support of her chair. I stared and then smiled at her ingenuity when I realized the towels were there so she could lean back and not pinch her long braid that easily brushed the seat bottom.

When I had made my choice—a horsehair bracelet braided in the four sacred colours of black, red, yellow, and white—she got out of her chair and showed me how to pull it tight without help from another, and then how to loosen it, using a piece of string. Her fingers were bent and twisted by arthritis, and I marvelled at her dexterity and perseverance in making such intricate art.

She had me practise the movements and, pleased with my progress, offered me the string when I was done. A small woman, she barely came up over my shoulder. She signalled a return to her chair by patting my arm and politely turning down an offer to have her picture taken.

* * *

There were times when I knew it all. I had all the answers, and if I didn't, I pretended to. It was an annoying stage for friends and family. I could picture the eye rolls behind my back when I'd correct someone or tune-up their ignorance.

I would use my smartphone to weaponize my righteousness, googling my way to "I told you so." People didn't like to be told they were wrong, and they definitely didn't like to be shamed. I certainly didn't, so I wasn't precisely sure how I got to the point where people would scatter when I entered the room.

Taking a big guess, I'd say my smartass need to show everyone how much I knew came from a lack of self-esteem, driven by childhood trauma, accelerated by fear enduring in anxiety. That was the short answer. A longer one was more than I wanted to dissect at the moment. *See, I've learned to stay out of the weeds and on point.*

Everyone would be particularly aggravated by me when I'd learned something new; regardless of the subject of the conversation or family agenda, I'd find a way to show them how smart I was. I'd talk and then talk some more, and I'd resent people who wanted to talk when I was talking.

I realized I was a know-it-all chatterbox when I found myself continually apologizing for correcting someone, for talking too much, and for repeating the same thing several times as if I were speaking to someone dumber than myself. My behaviour wasn't pretty, and if the saying, *I'd tell ya, but then I'd have to kill ya* was still socially correct, I'd have shot myself.

I acknowledged my self-loathing and understood it was another by-product of my trauma and the destructiveness I was exposed to as a child. But no violence was involved when I was shown the red path of my Algonquin Grandmothers. It came from love. I was grateful for the awakening to my community and for the ancestors who nudged me along to find my family. They reminded me I was able to walk the path in a good way, with a good heart and open mind.

A couple of years before COVID-19, I helped with a local youth circle, held in a community room at the town's arena. One day we were sharing thoughts about Wisdom and what it means. Wisdom is one of the Seven Grandfather or Grandmother Teachings or—for those who don't identify with the binary—the Seven Sacred Teachings. They are to be lived together, so to talk about one is to mention the others: Love, Respect, Honesty, Courage, Humility, and Truth. Some Nations would use Generosity instead of Truth, but I liked Truth. It allowed me to reflect on whether I was living the other teachings well. Was I being respectful? Was I open to love? Was I loving? Was I walking in humility? I have found when I followed the principles of the Seven Sacred Teachings my nature was grateful and generous.

Most kids believed Wisdom came from an accumulation of knowledge regardless of how you come to it. Smartphones were produced to show that wisdom was at our fingertips. Who needs a lifetime to accumulate knowledge? We have it all right here, and it fits in our pocket.

When we talked about age, the discussion focused on Wisdom as being accumulated knowledge over a lifetime of experience and how, because they were young, they could find information, but couldn't truly use it without the context gained from age and experience.

But was this truly the Wisdom we sought? Or was the understanding of what we knew just as important as what we didn't know? We discussed the idea of always looking at learning as being circular and infinite, just like the Medicine Wheel. But was Wisdom always going to be about learning new things, as opposed to being simply content with the awareness that there were things we didn't know nor needed to? One young man answered it would be good to look for the stuff you didn't know, for when you were "talking to the principal about, like, being suspended."

* * *

I didn't go to Star Lodge with the intention of writing a story about my experience. If I had, I would have offered Bear (Joel Babin, Waghoshig First Nation), the teacher and leader of Star Lodge, some tobacco and asked for his guidance and support. I have sent this story to Bear to read, and he gave me his blessing to go forward with it. Maarsii, meegwetch, thank you Bear.

People who have read this story asked lots of questions wanting to find out more. I purposely left out those things I felt weren't mine to tell. For me, ceremony requires attendance and reverence. Go to a lodge, talk to an Elder, attend ceremony, and experience it for yourself. The answers you find will fill your heart.

* * *

A few weeks after the sharing circle, I attended a four-day Star Lodge Ceremony east of Ottawa on land owned by my friends Carole and Eric. With Star Lodge, there were specific roles and dress protocols for women and men. Being Two Spirited, I was apprehensive about how I would be received, as I had been previously directed by an Elder to wear a skirt if I wanted to participate in their ceremony. I was ready to respectfully decline and leave the land if I had to wear one. I needn't have worried. Bear, the lodgekeeper and teacher, passed along the sentiment through my friend Julie to "Wear what you want, and do what you want." I took that to also mean to act respectfully within the larger ceremony protocol.

On the morning of my first day, the acreage was bustling with activity. It was warm for late September. The sun graced our faces and burnt the dew from the still-green grasses of the field we'd gathered in.

Near the long stacks of split firewood, Grandmother Ginette was sitting on a blanket with a young woman named Lisa and her two daughters, Jamika and Jaliah. Bear, with his gentle manner and seemingly always present smile, had just finished showing them how to scrape the inner bark off alders, and the blanket between them was covered with mounds of the small brown curls. Alder is one of the ingredients used for the smoking mixture loaded in the pipes for the sweat lodges.

Opposite, along the edge of the forest, Grandmother Liz was settled in a lawn chair, a bundle of sage in her lap. At her feet were several women of all ages and colours, chatting and laughing as they separated sage leaves from their stems. Sage was one of the medicines used to smudge, or cleanse, participants, sacred objects, the land, and the ceremonial grounds. It was also an ingredient in the smoking mixture.

I joined the multinational crew of men and women constructing the sweat lodge frame from twenty-eight sapling alders and maples. Ralph from Nova Scotia dug the same number of holes to anchor the saplings. Later, José, a lodgekeeper from Mexico, directed the bending, weaving, and tying together of the young trees to create the dome shape of the lodge. A young couple from Lithuania was tearing up strips of cloth. Youngsters hustled hot water in pots to be poured over the critical bends, while others bound the young trees together with coloured strips of cloth. Bear showed us how to create the four doorways of the lodge using two saplings for each door. He bent them to create half-moon shapes, and together as a group we pulled and weaved long maple saplings horizontally through the vertical supports to strengthen the frame.

The arrangement of the saplings in the structure created an eight-pointed star at its apex over a bowl-like depression that had been dug out of the earth in the centre of the round space below. A cedar wreath tied in the centre of the star created the doorway to the star world. The dome frame was covered with a cloth umbrella that was divided and sewn into six sections, each one a sacred colour of Star Lodge: yellow, red, green, blue, white, and violet. Many hands came together to finish the covering, layering on thick blankets, cloth and tarps to make the sweat lodge impervious to light.

Watching the building of the lodge was like watching a musical. A beautiful orchestration of strength and cooperation, people learning and creating with a reverence and a love for each other as well as for the land and its resources.

Four poles were dressed in coloured flags and raised in the four directions to honour the ceremonial grounds. The relationship between the lodge, altar, and fire was best pictured as an infinity symbol. A berm of sand representing the moon circled the fire at one end. The fire represented the sun. The opposite half was the circle made of the lodge itself, and where the two halves intertwined was a raised altar that marked the entrances to the sacred fire and to the sweat lodge. The simplicity and balance of the layout brought a flow of energy to the ceremony, one that reminded us of the endless possibilities we all carry.

The fire was built on a raised sand bed in a way I'd never seen. Two rows of split wood were laid parallel, about a foot apart, not quite four feet long, oriented north to south because, as Grandmother Liz said, it was the masculine direction. Stacked on top was a row of wood, creating a space below for kindling and bark, and above a cradle for the twenty-eight stones to be used in the lodge, known as the Grandmothers. The Grandmothers, arranged in a pyramid shape, were tented with more wood, and then a final row was added to close the top. Openings were left in the south and north ends of the stack to help with airflow.

The community of women, men, and children gathered in a circle around the fire to drum and sing while the youngest girl lit the fire. The birch bark crackled and spit loudly while wood smoke filled the air and coloured our clothes. The sacred fire would burn continuously and be used to heat up the Grandmothers for as many days as there was ceremony.

I joined the firekeepers—David, George, and Terry—and we set up our chairs under a shelter at the edge of the grounds. The men welcomed me fully. Like my being there wasn't anything out of the ordinary for them, and after an hour it felt like we had known each other for years. We easily slipped into the chores: tending the fire; handling the Grandmothers; taking direction from the lodgekeepers; passing sacred objects, medicines, and pipes in and out of the lodge; and hustling for a never-ending supply of water and wood needed for the ceremony.

I eagerly took on the task of looking after the pipes. Every person who came with a pipe would rest it on a stand, which was made of small branches supporting a long cross piece, erected on the altar. The pipe stayed there for the length of the ceremony or for however long the person was on the grounds.

David taught me that when the Grandmothers were hot enough from being in the fire, they'd be grey in colour. If left too long in the heat, they'd turn white and become more fragile, easily broken or cracked. When they were ready, a firekeeper called out loudly, "Lodgekeepers, Pipe Carriers, and women on their moon time," to let the people know it was time to come to the lodge for ceremony.

After the lodgekeepers were seated inside around the centre bowl, the Pipe Carriers filled the remaining space around it. Women on their moon time sat close to and behind the lodgekeeper that would be pouring the water. Moon-time women were cared for and honoured by others in ceremony in this way as life-givers in the community.

At the beginning of every lodge, five Grandmothers were sent in one at a time, greeted by a welcoming song. A helper would pick up and place the hot stones into the depression using a pair of deer antlers. They were arranged touching each other, one in the centre and then one in each of the four directions, starting with the east. After they were placed, the Grandmothers were sprinkled with medicines such as ground-up cedar, bear root, and sweetgrass.

The pipes were sent into the lodge in the order required so that no pipes crossed one another. After a pipe song was sung to the five directions that the stones were placed in, the pipes were smoked by those who carried them. Sweetgrass braids were held to the hot Grandmothers until they ignited, and then their smouldering ends were used to light the smoking mixture. Once smoked fully, the pipes were returned to the altar in the same order they went into the lodge.

Working with the sacred pipes was a special opportunity to take care of them. My job was to clean and load them, making them ready and available for ceremony. There were up to seven lodges a day, so it was a busy time. Over the four days in ceremony, several people came and sat with me to help or to take care of their own pipes. Some were chatty, while others would sit in quiet contemplation beside me as we recited prayers to accompany each pinch of mix.

Like the people who carried them, the pipes came in all different types and styles, shapes and colours. There were green turtles; black bears; white, green, and brown T-style pipes; and red and black L-shaped pipes. There was even one with a turtle laying on the round stone, like it was sunning itself on a surfaced log.

The stems were curved and straight, long and short, made of sumac and of other woods like cedar and maple. One was wrapped in bear fur, while most of the others were left plain.

It was after loading the pipes that I met Nathan. He was sitting in my chair chatting up George and David with a big smile. Nathan hung out for a couple of days, helping to tend the fire, and I came to grump at him several times: "Out of my chair. Your legs are younger than mine."

David finally told him, "If you wanted a chair like that to sit in, you should have brought one." It didn't deter Nathan, but he started to keep an eye out for me. When I got close, he'd jump out of my chair, relinquishing it with an exaggerated flourish and the occasional bow like some medieval member of a royal court.

I couldn't help but laugh, and over the days we all shared stories and teachings we'd learned with him and a couple of other younger men, Miguel and Ryan. The young men were all eager to help and learn, and to share what they had learned with us. It was always nice, especially at the end of a long day that usually started at three-thirty or four o'clock in the morning, to have young legs to load wood, carry water, and bring the Grandmothers from their nesting spot to ready them for ceremony.

One morning Carla, who was a Pipe Carrier, a Sundancer, and David's partner, asked me if I'd ever cleaned the pipes with a cedar bath. Bear wanted me to bathe them and asked Carla to approach me. I initially thought I'd done something wrong and was hesitant, but she was very graceful with her suggestions and generous with her guidance.

During an extended break between lodges, I set up a table, covered it with a wool blanket, laid out my medicines—a bear drum, a bear paw shaker, sage, and sweetgrass—and started a smudge. I'd found a deep, wide pan and layered the bottom with sprigs of cedar. I took apart the pipes, laid the stems on a red cloth, and put the pipestones in the pan on the bed of cedar. I'd heated up cedar water in a bucket by the fire, and when it was hot—close to boiling—I poured the water gently and slowly over the pipes in the pan.

After the stones soaked for ten minutes, I took them out one at a time and, using a pipe-cleaner I'd fashioned from a bear paw bone and coat hanger wire, dug out the softened residue in the bowls and air passages.

Miguel and Ryan asked to help, and after pulling up some extra chairs, we sat and cleaned pipes together for over an hour. Intent on our work, the space gradually quieted as people rested. A light wind rustled the leaves, and birdsong graced our work, lulling us into a spell.

Once we were happy with the cleaning, we used bear grease to coat the stones and then polished them with soft cloths. If the stems were restricted and needed cleaning, we heated up the ends of coat hanger wire by pushing them into the hot coals of the fire. Once they were red hot, we pushed them through the draw hole to burn out any restrictions. The stems were then greased and polished before the pipes were reassembled and placed back on the altar stand.

Miguel showed me the piece of soapstone he was working on to make his own pipe. He told me that Maggie, a Pipe Carrier who had helped me load pipes earlier in the day, was going to show him how to drill his holes later that evening. He was excited about that next big step.

Ryan shared that he was looking forward to receiving the vision that would be his pipe. "Did you carve your pipe?" he asked me.

My pipe is an effigy of a bear, carved so that the bear appears to be looking towards the one holding the pipe. "Yes, I carved it from stone that came from Enterprise, a small village near my home." Most of the pipestone is black. Shades of brown and grey, and small veins of white track through it.

I picked up my stem from the blanket. "The sumac for my stem came from my property." I liked to use sumac to carve stems because its soft centre was easy to push a heated wire through. "I mostly use sumac that has fallen down because during its life it gave us our life by filtering the air we breathe. After it fell, it provided cover for the little critters. And, in the end, it was feed for the beetles, and now it gives life and breath to the pipe." I showed Ryan and Miguel the random paths of beetle marks routed out of my stem. "To me, it represents that circle of life."

Miguel picked up the last stone, a white pipe. He was meticulous with the other stones, spending twice as long as Ryan and I did to get them just perfect. I reminded him of the beauty of transience and the perfection of imperfection. He nodded in a distracted way, keeping his focus on the pipestone.

Carla came to visit when we were almost finished. After her graceful guidance, she walked away to let me make the decision about bathing the pipes. She was very happy to see us all together.

Her pipe had a piece of bear hide wrapping the stem, and she told us that she removed it several times a year to bathe and clean it before dressing it lightly with bear grease before re-wrapping the stem. Carla was also determined to carve a pipe of a bear paw holding the bowl. She asked me about my bear paw shaker and if she could hold it.

The shaker was made from the rear paw of a bear cub that was hit by a car. I saw the cub when I came over a rise on Highway 17 just west of Rolphton. The cub was in the middle of the highway, and I pulled over to take it off the road. The Trans-Canada Highway was a major transportation route, and I didn't want him to suffer the indignity of being run over again and again.

He opened his eyes when I started to move him. Barely conscious and badly hurt, he was bleeding from a deep cut into his shoulder, which showed broken bone. He moaned when I picked him up off the asphalt and again when I laid him down on the gravel shoulder.

The young people who had hit him came back with a man in a truck, ready to take the bear. He left when told the cub was alive. The driver, a young man in his twenties, was holding a piece of his bumper, crying unabatedly. "I couldn't stop. I tried. It happened so fast." He paused and gulped. "I'm sorry. I'm so sorry." A young woman hugged him while his friend, a tall, lanky man around the same age, stood awkwardly with his hands shoved into his jeans, kicking rocks off the shoulder into the ditch.

"I'm sorry. It'll be okay. And it's good that you came back to check on him." I assured him that there was nothing he could have done differently and that if it was okay with them, I would take care of the little bear. He stuttered out, "Thank you," between deep, rattling breaths, the type that can only come from anguish. His lanky friend helped me swaddle the cub in towels, and together we lifted him into the back of my car.

I drove fifteen minutes to Deep River, where a constable met me at the edge of town in the parking lot of the old dairy. Constable Rick was sturdy looking with his vest and duty belt and was surprised to see me. I thought he was expecting a man with a bear in his truck, not a woman with a cub in her car.

The cub had unwrapped some of his swaddling and was trying to stretch free of the rest. He was disoriented, barely able to open his eyes, and moving in slow motion. Constable Rick took one of the towels and covered his head to calm him.

There were no wildlife services available in the area, and since it was a Sunday, Constable Rick spent several minutes on the phone trying to get a vet in the area to look at the cub. As I waited, I felt that he knew what the outcome would be, and that he was calling mostly for my benefit. Like he knew I was going to be okay with the decision to shoot him when it became obvious that we weren't going to find any help for him.

We drove behind the dairy and parked at the edge of the bush. I lifted the cub out of my car and carried him to where the grass was growing beyond the dirt of the lot, laid him down, and unwrapped the layers of towels. He moved his legs and opened his eyes when I stroked his head. "It's going to be okay." I laid loose tobacco on his head. "Meegwetch, thank you for your life, little one."

Constable Rick ended his suffering with a single shot after asking me to turn away. "He'll die instantly, but he'll spasm for a few seconds after."

In that moment, I was responsible for the little bear. He'd given me his life.

I wrapped him back up and brought him to Walt and Sandy's place, where we had a sacred fire and a pipe ceremony to see him off in a good way to the spirit world.

Walt stayed up all night to show me how to skin and scrape his hide. We took care of every piece of him, including driving his body kilometres into the bush. We heard the coyotes howling around four o'clock in the morning and assumed they'd found him.

I left after sunrise with his hide and paws. Walt would bury his skull to let the beetles clean it naturally before bringing it into his ceremonial space.

The cub spent some time in my freezer because I was afraid to work on him. He'd given me his life, and I needed to honour his spirit fully. My hesitation came from not wanting to ruin his hide or paws by making a mistake.

I worked through the anxiety by telling myself I only had good intentions, and one day when it felt good, I brought out one of his paws. It was the shaker I carried now, the one that Carla was holding and stroking softly.

I learned how to de-bone the paw to his claws by watching some videos, jokingly referred to by some friends as Kokum or Grandmother YouTube. While it took me longer than onscreen, I got it done. I was very pleased that I hadn't sliced through any hide while trimming around his finger bones to keep his claws in place. Afterwards, I packed his paw with pickling salt to pull out moisture and kill any bacteria.

Once the paw was dry, I rehydrated it with water and then trimmed and sewed the leg section to fit a piece of sumac. While it was still wet, I stuffed it with couscous and moulded it to the shape I wanted.

Several winters ago, I'd been unable to find some clean dry sand to use as stuffing, and after scrounging through my pantry, I'd discovered that couscous works well when shaping wet rawhide. The bonus with the small balls of pasta is that they also absorb some of the moisture of the hide, speeding up the dry time. And it was reusable—maybe not for dinner, but certainly for shaping shakers.

After a few days, I shook out the couscous and slowly added small stones, which I had picked from my driveway, to get the sound I wanted. Once tuned, I soaked the end of the leg just enough to be able to push the sumac into position for the handle. I then secured the hide to the sumac by wrapping and tying it with heavy black cotton thread.

I learned bears are powerful medicine, and they have many things to teach us if we pay attention. They have shown us where to forage and what plants and berries to eat. How hibernating is taking that time needed for recharging and healing. That a mother bear is a fierce protector of family and justice; she reminds us to draw on our inner strength to face our fears and difficulties with courage and to defend our beliefs.

The little cub taught me a lot. I learned how to skin and scrape his hide, how to debone his paws, and how to turn his ears and nose. I learned how to tan his head to make a medicine bag to hold my pipe. Lastly, I made a drum from his hide, keeping his fur on and wrapping it around a frame I made from steamed eastern white cedar.

Most importantly, the little bear taught me to be humbled with the gift of his life, to be grateful and generous, and to gift a part of him to those who helped me with his journey. His voice and spirit will be forever heard, not only through the shakers and the sound of the drum, but also through the telling of his story. I have often shared what I learned from him with others.

Carla and I were both dewy-eyed when I finished the story. Miguel and Ryan were sitting with their heads bowed. I re-lit the smudge, and Miguel turned his attention back to the stubborn corners of the white pipestone while Ryan hustled the last pipes over to rest on the altar before helping me clean up.

When I left Star Lodge, Carla gifted me with a salve of bear grease infused with all the medicines used in ceremony. I was very pleased and honoured when I came to understand how long and what kind of commitment it took for Carla to make the salve.

The last day Nathan was on the land, he came to say goodbye. After we hugged, he stood back with a big smile and laughed, "thanks for your chair. And for all the teachings you shared."

"You are welcome." After he walked a few steps away, I called out to him. When he turned, I spontaneously held my arms up and out to the side and told him, "I know nothing, but we know everything!"

He grinned. "Can I use that?"

"Of course, you can. All my relations."

When I said all my relations, I was talking about our relations with self, family, friends, and people. But I was also talking about being in kinship with the world we live in: the four-leggeds, the swimmers, the fliers, the crawlers, Mother Earth, the water, Father Sky, the tall standing ones, the plant world, the stars, the energies of Grandmother Moon and Grandfather Sun, the wind, the thunderers, the rain, the snow, and all the great mysteries lived and yet to be lived. Nothing is lesser than the other and each are vital to the whole. That is all our relations.

The Star Lodge ceremony was a big event in the life of a good friend. Bear passed the lodge on to Julie, and she will now be offering his teachings to the community, teachings which were passed to him by his mother, which were passed to her by...

* * *

During my time at Star Lodge, I saw Bear as an amazing teacher and guide, a generous man with a big heart and a happy smile. It was obvious he was devoted to his mom, Grandmother Liz. She had the same big heart, was strong, funny, generous, and courageous.

Not long ago Liz passed on to the spirit world; her contribution to the community was best said by Chief Juliet June Black of the Wahgoshig First Nation,

> *For years Elizabeth sat at the Door of the Star Lodge as hundreds of people crawled in and crawled out. She poured the Waters and blessed our Journeys, providing Sacred Space to renew our lives with songs and prayers as we received Instructions from the Star Ancestors. She sent her students to the Four Directions to share what they have learned just as she has. And throughout all these years she wove the strong beautiful blanket that is her Family and wrapped them in her Love.*
>
> All my relations.

CHAPTER 12
40 YEARS A VIKING

I HEADED SOUTH through the Black Hills towards Wind Cave National Park. I thought about stopping at the park—my upgraded park pass would let me in for free—but it was raining, and the clouds were heavy. The gloomy mood was made even darker by the presence of the forest, a being in and of itself.

Uninterested in visiting or stopping, I continued driving through the Buffalo Gap and Oglala grasslands before turning north, eventually landing on Highway 79. I stopped briefly to explore the very small town of Buffalo Gap.

It was obvious the Last Chance Saloon had its last chance. It sat in a nest of structures and small houses that look unused, if not abandoned, but for the cut and trimmed grass surrounding the buildings. I looked across the street towards city hall, a small red building made of sandstone blocks. If it weren't for a light on inside, I would have thought it abandoned as well.

I took in the Trading Post. A fairly new large building, surrounded by furniture and fixtures, it advertised a collection of Native American and western art, collectables, and antiques for sale.

The building was crowded, making for narrow aisles and packed shelves. Above the rows sat animal pieces and heads, most with antlers, looking out from the walls; faux Indian headdresses hung off the same hooks as sombreros, ball caps, and cowboy hats. Sunglasses, star quilts, coyote pelts, lanterns, chairs, rotating fans, cowboy boots, umbrellas, flocks of stuffed birds, and all the other usual flea market inhabitants filled the space.

It was my kind of beautiful, and I walked around and through displays for a half hour or more, looking at and picking up stuff. Even though I was tempted to purchase a lantern for camping, I couldn't. There wasn't one other person in the store, and I searched but couldn't find a counter to ring a bell at or yell "Hello!" from.

There was a small office-like room in the corner by the entrance, sectioned off with some cheap strand board, but it was empty. I heard muted voices from somewhere in the back of the building that could have been a radio, but I didn't have the courage to open the door or go looking. *Old lady queer last seen alive in Buffalo Gap. One black Ford Edge for sale.*

I walked around the building to a side porch that protected chairs, filing cabinets, and a gate sign advertising the Buffalo Gap Cemetery. I twirled around—not with dizzying speed, but slowly. I saw cars, houses, barns, and sheds, but not one single person. Not even a dog had greeted me. It was starting to feel right spooky. This was the type of place Paula warned me to stay away from. I walked back to the Edge, hopped in and locked the doors.

I drove out of Buffalo Gap and pulled into the Flying J truck stop in Hermosa. I had a sandwich for dinner in the diner, which Skinny Bitch got on at me about. *You know that's bread, right?* I was tired and lonely, and in defiance, Fat Chick hoovered three Reese's peanut butter cups before climbing into the Ford.

* * *

The cold had crept in and laid itself as frost in the bottom corners of the leaky windows and doors of the cottage. Feeling the chill, she went to stand in front of the woodstove and wondered how the day would end. 'I'm afraid for her,' she thought, looking towards the table where the iPhone was sitting. She was waiting for a message and had only now realized how desperate she was for good news. We deserved it. Every day of not knowing had increased her anxiety, and the tension strung across her chest and gut was so taut she'd be afraid to pluck the strings even if they were available to her. She had hidden the tension because she didn't want to add to the stress that had permeated their lives these last days with a growing persistence.

She wondered if she was just being selfish, and if she only wanted it to be good news because then she wouldn't have to deal with her dark moods and snappiness. Her sullenness had drowned the past few weeks in a muttering silence, and she didn't want to live with any more of it. She had tried to be supportive and kind. But in a way, she'd rather be snapped at. It was easier to confront a slight from her with her own snappiness than deal with a glancing expression or a piercing stare that was full of something she couldn't define.

She sighed loudly. She acknowledged it had been an uncertain time for them both. The manic energy of wishing for good news in one moment was always followed by the darkness of trampled hopes in the next. It had been an unpredictable rollercoaster. An up separated from a down by a second or by an hour or by a day. She thought of the possible bad news, and fear flicked at a string low in her belly, accelerating her heart rate and breathing.

She wished the phone would ding its notification so at least it would be over. In her pragmatism she was certain it would be better to deal with what they knew than what they didn't know. *It is what it is.* It should be simpler, put a problem on the table and start fixing it. You paid your bill, made up a schedule, called for a prescription, went to the bank, and picked up groceries. She'd have it all solved in an hour, all done, no problem.

Her back warm, she went over and sat on the couch, but not before glancing again at the table where the phone sat, silent. Her nanny had a saying, something about a watched pot not boiling. She never cooked—she never wanted to—but the principle still applied. *Maybe it will ding if I stop looking over at it.* She vowed not to turn and check it for the next five minutes.

A self-help book about healing chakras laid on top of a pile of local phone books and recreational guides. They were stacked on an antique wooden army trunk they picked up at a local garage sale and used as a coffee table. Its sides were full of holes plugged with rounds of softwood, making them believe it had been used for more than transporting personal belongings. She picked up the book, one of many she always had at hand, and she tried to find her way through a paragraph. Minutes later, after losing focus several times, she dropped the book back onto the trunk in frustration.

A dark, moving shadow captured her attention. Through the large window facing the lake, she saw a black squirrel jumping from the branches of one oak to another, making its way through the forest. She watched it run up a branch that would seem impossible to travel on and then jump to another, barely clinging to its bark before finding purchase and scampering up its limb. It disappeared into a cluster of waving branches, getting smaller and smaller.

She unconsciously twisted and snapped the mala beads circling her wrist and thought back to dinner last night. Looking across the table, she could see the tiredness in her eyes, how strands of hope and fear had braided her brow, and the set of stress in her jaw. She could hear her teeth grinding last night through the few hours of sleep they managed to get. The hours seemed less and less with each passing night.

The search for answers had always percolated in half-hearted spurts through the seventeen years she had known her father's name. She had grown used to the "here we go again" routine of it all, knowing it'd only go so far before ebbing and stopping as abruptly as it started. That was what always happened, until now. Now it was real.

She wished she could wipe away the pain and uncertainty this last push for a resolution had brought into their lives. Contrary to her habit of always trying to avoid any discomfort, she decided that she might even keep some of it for herself if she really had to. She tried to remember what she had read recently about the law of attraction; it didn't make that much of an impression, but she hoped she had been on the right frequency to manifest good news.

She didn't know if it had been five minutes or not, but she wanted to turn around and stare at the device, to somehow consciously force it to give her what she wanted. She lifted herself from the couch and went to the stove, adding another length of wood to the box. She turned to see the phone and stood on the hearth, rubbing her arms. She wondered if it really was this cold in the cottage—should she be looking for an open window? Or was it fear driving her chills?

She turned the phone on this morning, because she rarely did, and it had become a point of friction between them. *Why have a phone if you're not going to have it turned on? And what happens if it's an emergency or if I just need to talk to you?*

The phone pinged. Chords thrummed through her body with such a rush that goosebumps raised the hair on her arms. She quickly walked over and stared at it. Its notification banner was still visible. "It's here," she whispered, and then she repeated the words, raising her voice as though she didn't hear herself the first time. "It's here."

The vibrations drifted down and settled in her stomach. She picked up the phone; it should have felt heavier, she thought, for the news it was carrying. She looked out the back window towards the sauna. She could see the smoke from the stainless-steel chimney and remembered the days she helped her build it. She'd always been that way, driven and a dreamer, always creating and building something or looking for the next adventure. She hoped those dreams wouldn't be trampled today.

Her fingers pecked out her password, a familiar variation of all her passcodes. She tapped the email icon, and there it was, bold type in the subject line. She breathed deeply several times, like she was taught at the yoga studio, and touched the screen to open the message. The news was in an attachment.

Grabbing her coat, she slipped her feet into her boots and opened the door. She walked up the driveway, holding her coat closed with one hand and gripping the phone with the other. She opened the outer door to the sauna, stepped into the alcove, and knocked on the pine-covered inner door. Within moments the door opens. She was naked.

"It's here," she said, holding the phone up.

"Let me get my towel."

They stood in the driveway facing each other. She'd wrapped a towel around herself and tucked a corner into an armpit. The echo of a woodpecker reached them just as a light wind swept the top of the snow on the bank.

She kept her expression neutral and solemnly handed the phone to her. She knew the news but didn't want her to know she knew.

She saw her apprehension; saw how she was fighting the hope that had crept into her features. Steam was rising off her wet hair and the damp skin of her shoulders and arms. She saw her shaking as she worked the phone. Zipping up her jacket, she waited.

She reached out for her as the towel slipped off, and she crumpled. Her knees struck the ground before she laid her head in the snow in front of her. Her naked back steamed. A low moan escaped her prostration.

* * *

Three weeks earlier.

Leona leaned towards me, whispering urgently, "I found him."

I stretched down the long table towards her. "What?"

"I found him."

I carefully moved my chair back to avoid disturbing a group of researchers at the other end of our joined tables. We were in the National Archives of Canada. I took a few careful steps towards Leona and hovered over her shoulder. She pushed her finger slowly up the city directory page, stopping at a name, and twisted her head to look up at me. Her round face brimmed with excitement. "It's him. It's got to be him. It all fits."

I bent over to get a closer look at the shapes of the black letters on the newsprint-type paper. My eyes narrowed, focusing on the words. I fell into the chair beside her and pulled the directory towards me. I carefully read the details of the two lines, again and again. They didn't seem like much. They were insignificant, really—just two simple lines of black ink describing a man among thousands of men. A man that could be my father.

I held my breath and touched the letters, rubbing them softly, wanting them to rise and take shape so I could feel them, maybe even feel him. My mind was full. *Who is this man?* Besides his name, Bev was short on details, and I had so many questions, none of which she could have answered. *Is he wiry, big, short, or tall? Does he have dark hair or light hair? What kind of man is he—kind or hard? Is he tough? Is he funny or strict?*

I bent closer and inhaled the scents of aged paper and the dried glue of the binding and imagined cologne after a fresh shave. *Or is there another scent I should think of instead? A mixture of oil and fuel, or fresh-sawn wood, or the staleness of old booze and cigarettes?* My fingers rubbed the letters lightly. *Would he like me touching him?* I released my breath in a long, slow exhale. Shivers ran up my arms and over my shoulders, tingling my hairline. "You're right. It's him."

When I turned back to Leona, her smile was radiant. If she could have, I was sure she'd be up and bouncing and shouting her joy. Years of arthritis made Paula's aunt dependent on a walker some days. Today was one of them. I pulled her into a tight, fierce hug over the arms of the chairs between us.

"I can't believe we found him."

"I know, me neither."

We straightened out of the hug and looked at each other with big foolish happy grins.

"After finding nothing yesterday, I thought he didn't exist. I thought Bev had lied to me again," I confessed. We had enthusiastically started the search the day before after I teased Leona about only needing her for her gimp parking pass, which practically assured us of prime parking near the entrance to the archives. The day ended with both of us tired, but not so much as to prevent making plans for a return trip.

"I know, sweetie. Isn't it exciting?"

Leona dropped me at home, and I immediately went online. Within a few keystrokes, I found his obituary. Marcus Turcotte died several years ago, passing peacefully in his eighty-sixth year. I pulled my chair as close as I could to my desk to peer at his picture. It was a black-and-white photo of him sitting in a chair backed by a tree beside a lake. A summer shot, I'd say, as he was in short sleeves. He was wearing a hat over his short white hair, and he was thick through his face, neck, and chest. The type of fleshiness men built with age, a love of home-cooked comfort food, and a slowing down in later years. I would guess his age at late sixties or early seventies.

The obituary writer described his passion for country music and said he loved to fish and hunt. It was what you would expect from boys who became men in the rough hard-working communities and wild bush of Northern Ontario.

Marcus was looking sideways towards the camera through tinted aviator glasses sitting on an almost bulbous nose. His expression was difficult to read. He wasn't smiling and didn't look happy someone had taken his picture, but neither did he seem annoyed. It might have been one of those looks people put on to give them the impression of being pissed, even though they were really just screwing with you and were laughing inside.

Would he have looked at me like that if he had known me? Or, considering where I came from, would he have been pissed at me for showing up after all the years? Either way would be fitting. His presence in my life, like with that low-resolution black-and-white picture of him, was always floating around, never fully realized until that moment. And even though the image was dim, my first impression of Marcus, the man named by my mom as my father, was of a man's man, rugged and tough-looking.

I leaned back in my chair. Emotions rose. I wiped my cheeks roughly with my hands. I started to get angry. Not at him, but at myself for feeling something. For investing my hopes in a future with a man I knew only as a name, and then as a picture. And it turned out that he's fucking dead. I became the little girl looking for someone to love and care for her. It wasn't that I didn't want to feel. I did, but I wanted to feel normal and settled. I didn't want to feel so much hope that the idea of failure would bring unworthiness and fears of rejection. I tried the opposite; I tried to feel the wonder and the joy of finding him, but I couldn't get there then. The fear wouldn't acquiesce.

Marcus was a husband and father of four children, two boys and two girls. Questions slide through and around. *Are these my half brothers and sisters? Will they want to know me? What would it be like to have new sisters and brothers? They won't want to know me.*

My wish for Marcus to be real was held captive in the honesty of my mom, and her truth had always been a shifting landscape. There was no blame in that statement. My brothers and I learned to live with my mom's excuses, fluid storytelling, and rearrangement of time and circumstances. It was how she survived and coped in a violent marriage, and when I saw myself and my brothers re-enacting similar behaviour over time, I knew we learned from the best.

After more online searching, I found the obituary of Marcus's oldest son, Vincent, who left this world in his late forties. There was no picture of the man who might have been my brother. All the familiar family names were there. He was extensively involved in several communities through his work, and I softened for him and his family when the obituary ended with an affectionate *luv always!*

I was unable to find any online presence for any of Marcus's other children, but Vincent's wife had remarried, and after following the trail of several online obituaries of her family, I found a woman on Facebook I believed to be her. She used three names—two married ones and her maiden name. I was ninety-nine percent certain she was my sister-in-law Marie.

I sat in my chair, clicking through Marie's life on Facebook, understanding this could still all be my fantasy. The black-and-white picture of a man named Marcus was really a conjuring of my desires and imagination, mixed with a tenuous construct made up and passed on to me by my mom. I could see her picking a name on a random page out of a telephone book, tearing it out, crumpling it up in her fist, and air balling it to me. I wouldn't blame her if she made it all up to pacify my anger at her for being unfaithful. I wasn't angry at her because of her duplicity, it was her selfishness in keeping it from me. For forty years, I thought I was a Viking. When people asked, I'd proudly tell them my grandparents had emigrated from Denmark. I often daydreamed about visiting Copenhagen and exploring the Nordic countries. It was all a lie, and I was pissed.

But to be fair, at the time of her confession, she was ill with cancer and the effects of chemotherapy. She was fighting for her life. If I were in the same spot, I'd have possibly done the same: cast out something, anything, to appease me and get some rest. I might have chosen something a bit beefier, like stuffing the paper into a dog's Kong and throwing it out into the middle of the lake—*Chase that, bitches*.

It meant that all of this—these last years, months, days, and then hours spent sitting in my chair ruminating, chewing fingernails, sweat running down behind my ears—could be a fairy tale based on the belief that my mom was telling me the honest, actual truth, and not her convenient, get-out-of-trouble storytelling truth. A truth I've held on to for almost seventeen years. I was never ready for the answers that trying to find Marcus would bring until now. I didn't want to face the idea that Bev might have lied to me; I didn't want to feel the betrayal. I wanted to believe that in the end, when she was dying, she loved me, and in her love, she could only offer the truth. It was easier for me to live with the idea of a Marcus than live with the possibility of not ever knowing him.

I really wished I'd had the courage when I was fifteen, or even ten years younger, to go chasing him down, but I didn't. I was a coward. I was afraid to find the truth. I was afraid then, and it made me doubt every decision or lack thereof. I deserved to know the truth of my creation. I knew that, and I felt it. I had no control over any decisions that led to my conception. Logically, I knew my being alive was not my fault and I wasn't the problem. But I felt like I was the problem, that somehow the anxiety, stress, and indecision was my fault. My rational self told me this was irrational thinking, and I tried to get to the other side of it, but it always came looping back.

After mindlessly clicking links, circling around the obituaries, seeking out any news of the Turcotte family online, and chewing my nails for an hour, I messaged Marie on Facebook asking if she was married to Vincent Turcotte and if she was the daughter-in-law of Marcus. Every keystroke registered like a hole punch snapping through tin.

After a couple of hours, I got a very tentative reply: *Who are you and why do you want to know?* I responded, suggesting that my mother knew Marcus. I said that I wasn't comfortable messaging over Facebook, but if she could give me her email address, I'd like to tell her a story.

I wrote a draft of an email and read it over and over. I changed a comma, and then I re-read it. Then I changed one word and re-read it again. Then I changed the tone and re-read it. Finally, I changed the salutation and re-read it.

I wasn't sure there was any manual or method on how to land in people's lives with a fifty-seven-year-old story of infidelity and betrayal. The idea of disrupting lives, interfering with a family's understanding of who they were, who their patriarch was, distressed me. *What if I'm wrong? People may get hurt.* Actually, it was very likely that people would get hurt, but I'd have no answers if I didn't press send. If the landing was going to be rough, then it was going to be rough. I hoped I was ready for whatever was coming. I hovered the cursor over the send button, breathed out loudly, and when I decided to leave it all up to the great mystery we lived in, I pressed send.

> Hi Marie,
> Thanks so much for receiving my note and "listening" to my story. I've composed this email in my head a number of times today and finally decided I'd just get down to it.
>
> My name is Lorrie Jorgensen. I'm fifty-seven years old, and I was born in Sudbury in 1959. I lived there until I was three, and then my family moved to Deep River, where I grew up. My parents were Eric and Beverly Jorgensen (nee Potvin), and I have three

brothers. I moved to Ottawa when I was seventeen and have lived in the area since.

In 1999, when I was thirty-nine, Eric went to trial for incest, sexual assault, and rape in Pembroke. The court asked for DNA evidence to determine whether Eric was my biological father, as the law at the time of the offences (in the sixties and seventies) required that the offender and victim be blood relatives. The DNA results proved that Eric was not my biological father.

It's very hard to describe how I felt at the time—shocked, angry, sad, and betrayed. I had no idea, nor was I ever given the slightest hint, that Eric was not my biological father. My mom kept this secret for almost forty years. Right before the results of the test were to be released, she told me my real father was Marcus Turcotte, who worked for the city of Sudbury. Let's say I've had some unresolved mother issues since.

I've also had Marcus Turcotte's name in my head for almost eighteen years. It's taken time for me to heal, process my feelings, gather strength, and finally work up the confidence and courage to make some inquiries. I can't ask my mom for any more details because she died within two years of the trial in 2001. She was sixty-two and had been sick for almost five years with colon cancer.

So, I went with my friend Leona to the national archives to look through the Sudbury city directories to confirm my mom's claim (or not). The directories list the male resident, his spouse if he's married, his type of employment, and his address. We were off track at first because I had written his name down as Mark Turcotte—my mom told me his name over the phone—and having lived so close to Hull I made the assumption it was the French version of Marc. It was like looking for a ghost, but once we discovered a Marcus Turcotte who worked at the city of Sudbury during the fifties and on—there were only a handful of Turcottes at the time, not like today—all the pieces came together. I imagine people called him the anglicized version of Mark, which sounds like Marcus.

I was also able to confirm from the directories that my mom, Eric, and Marcus all lived in Sudbury around the time of my conception and birth. Eric went missing for a year as he had gone to Halifax with the Navy. This was during the same timeframe that my mom said she was intimate with Marcus.

So, how did I come to get in touch with you? After finding Marcus's full name, I googled it and found his obituary. The information I found fit the Marcus Turcotte from the directories. From there I went through a process of googling names and places and followed a thread through several obituaries. This brought me to you. The use of your three last names together made the jumps fairly easy to make. I then found and messaged you on Facebook. Thank you for responding. It means a lot.

This past summer I went out west to Alberta to research the Potvin side of my family. My great-grandfather homesteaded near Wainwright in the early 1900s. I found the original homestead. It was amazing and heartening to walk the same land as my grandmothers and mother would have as a child.

My motivation for reaching out to you is for help with my mom's story. True or not, it is now my story, and I'd like to know the ending, regardless of the outcome. Please know I'm not looking to "crash" into people's lives, nor to cause anyone grief or harm. I'm only looking for guidance with some possible next steps.

Sit with this for as long as you need, and when you are ready, at a time that works for you, please get in touch.

Thanks for listening,

Lorrie J.

* * *

Within a few hours, I received a response from Marie. I could tell she was a kind person. Her soft language and gentleness helped to lessen my anxiety. She accepted my story and told me she would reach out to the family.

It was early the next day when Marie messaged me back. When I got her response, I was sitting at my desk, distracted and half-listening to a news program I tuned into, refreshing my email every time a commercial came on.

She told me she was able to connect with Marcus's oldest daughter to discuss my story. Marie told me my mom's story was quite possible. She knew there was some trouble in the family at the time, but she didn't know any more than that. She ended the note by saying someone from the family would be in touch.

Later in the day, I got an email from Marcus's youngest daughter. It was brief, abrupt, and to the point: *I hear you are looking for your father. Before going further, the family would like a DNA test.* She asked for my phone number and told me her sister Denise would be in touch.

That response was not unexpected, and while I could understand the tone and wariness of the message, I was happy there was mention of DNA testing. It was the only authentic way to prove or disprove Bev's story.

While I waited for Denise to call, the negative tone of the email took root, and I started to feel anxious. It sounded like I had made some people unhappy. I paced, watched some television, and spent time online googling random subjects. The dogs really should have been walked, but I didn't want to be away from the house.

The phone rang, and I wished we'd paid the extra five bucks for call display. It rang twice before I picked up. A throaty, warm voice asked for me, and when I responded, she continued, "So how are you doing with all this? Are you okay?" The tension gripping my heart drained away. I knew immediately I was going to be safe. It was going to be okay.

Denise told me that the family was in turmoil at the time. She was ten years old and was quite aware of the fighting. She was especially tuned into her mother's unhappiness. Her mother was pregnant, and her father was frequently absent, and she knew something was wrong. She believed it was very possible that her father was my father.

I knew she had gotten a copy of the email, but I re-tell some of my story anyway. Afterwards, she said, "So, Marcus Turcotte had a child out of wedlock." Her tone was more than just a statement. It had an edge to it. I would come to understand later that Marcus had shunned Denise for the very same indiscretion that he himself may have committed.

She asked if Marcus had ever seen me. I told her my mom had sent me some pages copied from her journal. In them, she described him looking at me in my crib when I was a newborn. She wrote, *It was the last time he'd ever see his little baby girl.* My mom also wrote that it was the happiest day of her life. I'm not sure whether she wrote that for me or for her, but knowing the violence she endured in her marriage to Eric, it very well could have been the happiest day of her life.

Denise offered to tell me more about Marcus, and she also shared a little more about herself. It was heartening to hear her say, "I treat people the way I want to be treated."

My mouth was dry, and my breath caught. "I don't want to know too much right now." I was on the verge of tears and took a deep breath. "I'd rather wait until we know for sure." I didn't tell her how afraid I was. Scared that this would all just end up being a good story for their family to laugh about around the table at Christmas dinner. *Do you remember when that crazy woman got in touch about Dad being her father?*

I arranged for the DNA testing. The technology was readily available and reasonably affordable. The company divided the test kit, mailed one half to Denise and the other half to me. I followed the instructions impeccably and imagined Denise doing the same a few hundred miles away.

I flashed back to my first DNA test. It was a swab test, just like the one on the counter in front of me, done by a man in a white lab coat. At the time, the push of the tip against the inside of my cheek felt like an assault. It felt like another one of Eric's violations. Like he was still in control of my body, and there was no escaping him.

Denise called to tell me she had sent off her half of the test kit by express post. I replied I had done the same. She offered again to share some Marcus stories, and I told her I appreciated her belief and trust, but I couldn't hear them yet. I sensed she would have liked to talk some more, but I begged off the phone.

The results were guaranteed to arrive within seven to ten business days. Paula and I decided to take a few days and headed up to the lake to try and relax. We got the news on a Friday.

* * *

I was naked, on my knees, when I looked up at her. Tears joined the sweat stinging my eyes. "Bev told the truth. He's my father." I handed the phone to Paula, and she helped me up before grabbing the towel to wrap around me.

"I need to call Denise."

She picked up quickly as she had when responding to all my calls. We were tentative and somewhat muted as we talked about the result. It was obvious we both wanted to be somewhere else sharing and debriefing the news. We ended the call quickly.

I hung up the phone. Was there a greeting card for this kind of news? *Congratulations on the birth of your new half-sister!* Or was there a type of party you could throw? We could have a big banner proclaiming *Welcome to this half of the family! Yeah Lorrie!* Too corny? How about a gender reveal celebration? Was there one for butch?

I sat and stared at the results. I was comforted by the narrative that described analysis, platforms, data, chain of custody, methods, and quality assurance. It was full of big and important words like quintillion, authenticated by a PhD using ISO numbers and several acronyms for standards I had never heard of. There was even a case number.

DNA testing was done to determine siblingship of the alleged siblings. Based on testing results obtained from analyses of the DNA loci listed, the probability of half-siblingship is 99.9%.

CHAPTER 13
40 YEARS CONTINUED

THE NEXT MORNING WAS CLOUDY, cold, and damp. I sat in the Edge with a fresh hot coffee from the diner and turned on the heated seat. I unfolded the map and considered where I might leap to next. I sighed heavily. The leapfrog game was getting tiring, I was far from home, and I was alone—just me and the Edge. I was grateful for my car. It was the first brand new vehicle I'd ever had, and I wouldn't have gone on this trip but for its newness and dependability.

It was Paula who convinced me that, at fifty-four, I deserved a new vehicle. It was a big commitment, and I stressed over my options for a month before deciding on the Ford. The salesman had to practically push me off the lot the day I picked it up. I was afraid because it felt like I was stealing it, like I had no right to be driving a nice, fancy new car. The funny thing was that Paula never really took to the Edge.

I looked at the time to check if it was too early to send her a text. It was.

Perhaps I was just tired from the hot flashes that had interrupted my sleep—probably caused by the Reese's. *It's not like I didn't warn you.*

When I left the truck stop, I turned right and then left onto Highway 40 and travelled southeast towards the Pine Ridge Reservation.

I entered the Oglala Lakota Nation at Red Shirt. Its name arranged out in letters on the slope of a hill to my right. The land was mostly rolling plains with dry grasses and some patches of dark shrubs. The sky had broken, and blue tracts started to appear among the lingering greys of the cloud cover.

Gradually, the grassland started to break away from itself, creating gulches and depressions. It was like the earth had suddenly fallen away in places. I couldn't seem to take my eyes away from the changing landscape. Soon there were no plains, only miles and miles of deep gorges, which turned into even deeper valleys, and switchbacks surrounding the occasional grass-topped butte. The Badlands.

I pulled over, parked with the wheels turned like I was in a Ford commercial, walked down to the edge of a gully, and sat. The erosion of time past was captured by the exposed sediment layers of the valley walls. The aura of silence, desolation, and wildness was ancient, and soon I got lost in my thoughts. I thought about how sacred the land was, how barren and prehistoric it felt. The lands were history in and of themselves, formations clawed from the earth that didn't seem to be of this world.

Reluctantly, I headed back to the Edge and continued driving east. I passed plots of land where dirt driveways threaded through the grassland, leading to small houses and trailers, most surrounded by the quiet, rusted carcasses of trucks and cars.

The desolation, which stretched for miles and miles, and the ethereal beauty of the country were remarkable and inescapable. I drove through a rise of buttes and then into a copse of trees that marked the land of the Red Cloud Indian School.

The buildings on campus were a mix of early finishes (red brick, concrete block, and plaster) and modern-style ones (steel, brick, and stucco). I recognized the geometric patterns from the Indian Museum at Crazy Horse painted on the pale yellow concrete of a building addition. White and black lines defined rectangles and triangles of bright red and blue.

The complex was quiet. Several cars were in the parking lot, but there was no activity, not a soul bustling about. There was a large sign paying homage to Chief Red Cloud. I read about his victories, defeats, and final role as a peacekeeper for his people. His grave was two hundred feet east of the sign. I trudged up the wide path that led to a flattened rise.

It was clear the cemetery was Catholic. The school was originally founded as the Holy Rosary Mission. A large white cross with a crucified Jesus dominated the plot where wild grasses have grown up and around some markers. It seemed fitting—Mother Earth was gradually absorbing the remains within the gentle sway of her grasses.

Even though the influence of the Church dominated the plots, there were subtle signs of the Sioux peoples. A set of wooden crosses, side by side, marked twin boys. The four directions of the medicine wheel, represented by coloured triangles, were painted on each white cross. Several gravestones and markers were graced with artificial flowers, solar lamps, and small mementos like angels and rocks.

The largest grave belonged to Red Cloud. He was named after the ball of fire from a meteorite that passed over Sioux country in 1822, the year of his birth. Red Cloud was Oglala Sioux from the Bear people band known as "Badfaces." His elevated tomb was enclosed by a white picket fence. A substantial granite cross on a triangular base rose above a mixed-stone top covering his tomb.

Below the cross was an inlaid circle carving in white stone. It showed Red Cloud wearing a headdress. I looked over the flat top and saw offerings of stones, crosses, rosary beads, bracelets, and cigarettes. There were also hoops of grasses, sage, and twigs bound with red cloth laying among the artefacts. I squinted. *Could it be?* Yes, it was a hacky sack, flattened and faded.

A simple white wooden cross, set into the grass beside his tomb, marked the grave of his wife Mary Red Cloud, also known as Pretty Owl. Biographers had remarked that it was Pretty Owl who was, with her determined and strong personality, the one in charge of the household.

I continued past Red Cloud's grave, beyond rows of modern and modest red gravestones. I soon came to a divided collection of markers for the Sisters and Brothers who toiled in the Jesuit ministry that founded the mission school in 1888. Facing the crucified Jesus that dominated the space, the Sisters were buried on my right, and the Brothers were interred to my left.

The graves of the Brothers swept by and around Jesus like an arc before fading into the wild grasses beyond the tall cross. The Brothers' places were marked with white stone crosses on sturdy stone bases. They were more substantive and descriptive than the simple iron markers of their Sisters. The crosses on top were etched with the Christogram symbol of the Society of Jesus. The stone below gave their full name and dates for their birth, entry into the Lord's service, and discharge of their service to Him upon their death.

I was drawn to the simple iron crosses of the Sisters. Most were painted silver, and they all had a patina of rust over the iron—some more afflicted than others. These Christian crosses were beautifully cast, elegant with scrollwork and embellished on the ends of the arms and vertical points. Some had a crucified Christ on the side opposite their dedication. I lightly touched them and rubbed my fingers along the rusted edges. They were exquisite and humble. That they were made of iron and steel was much more meaningful to me than the rigid stone blocks used for their Brothers.

Metal plaques, which were screwed to the centre of the crosses, described the women in an identical pattern; they begin with *Sister M.* and then indicated the last name of the woman. The crosses included their date of death, age at death, and the date they professed their life to the service of the Lord. There were no birth dates, although age at death was written. I supposed it was the Church's view that the date they began their service was their true birth date, unlike the men an aisle over.

Death in the Mission's early years didn't discriminate. While there were Sisters in their seventies and eighties, there were also Sisters who died in their twenties and thirties, having only dedicated their lives to service for four years, eight years, and in one instance, professed only eight months.

I looked around one last time at the swaying grasses beyond the flattened rise and gave thanks for the ancestors and all my relations before I made my way down the hill back towards the campus.

I decided to visit the gift shop. A sign on the door says in Sioux: *Tanyá yahí kštó/yeló. Thimá hiyú we/wo*. A line below translated: *It's good that you're here. Come inside.*

I was greeted by an enthusiastic young man. "Please look around and let me know if you need any help." He shared he was busy working on an upcoming art show and that they were short-staffed because they were also busy reorganizing the heritage centre, which was closed.

The gift shop was small, and the selection was even smaller. It only took a few minutes to view the jewellery, beadwork, quilts, and quillwork. All were exceptionally crafted, and I purchased a couple of quillwork pieces as gifts for friends.

At the cash, the young man assured me that the centre only purchased traditional artwork directly from Lakota artists. The gift shop had buying days twice a year for community members to come to the campus with their creations.

It was mid-morning when I drove into Pine Ridge. Small shrubs and weeds sprouted from cracks in the concrete sidewalks. Trees—some of which were dead but still standing—provided cover for an eclectic mix of structures. Water tanks rose above the hydro poles and lines.

Needing gas, ice for my cooler, and a coffee, I stopped at Big Bat's. A colourful sign to the left of the double-entry glass doors announced that Big Bat's loyalty program was coming soon. Posters advertising Marlboro and Newport "Pick Your Pleasure" cigarettes took up most of the window space on the left door.

I entered the shop and was immediately surprised, taken aback by cigarette smoke. In the diner area, several people were sitting at tables and along the counter. Out of the six or seven people I saw, only two didn't seem to have a lit cigarette, either smouldering in front of them in an ashtray or stuck between their lips or fingers.

My surprise came from working and living in Ottawa, where smoking had already been banned from community and shared spaces for well over fifteen years. Laws have been developed since to extend non-smoking areas thirty feet from building entrances, and it was now illegal for adults to smoke in a car with a child under the age of sixteen in Ontario.

Some of the Elders I knew who smoked said they needed to "smudge their lungs"—a spirited, light way to explain their addiction. I've stood beside them and others inhaling the wafts of smoke from the lit ends of their cigarettes, and there were times long after I quit that I still reached for the chest pocket of my coveralls to grab my pack of smokes.

The rest of the store offered the usual fare: chips, pretzels, and chocolate bars. Bags of candy jammed the shelves. At the Flying J, a person could pick up a huge barrel-sized coffee and muffins the size of a softball; here, the soda machine advertised a forty-four-ounce cup for $1.49. I did the math quickly and came to five and a half cups, over a litre of pop. Refills were even cheaper. Damn.

I balanced a coffee with a bag of ice and tucked myself into the Edge. Before I could shift into drive, a man with long black hair knocked heavily on the door glass. I powered down the window. He was swaying and looking around the lot, back and forth, and then his attention came back to me like he'd forgotten I was there. He asked for money. I held my wallet in my hand when I told him I didn't have any cash. My stomach lurched when he stared at it, and I dropped the wallet to my thigh out of sight. After a moment, he backed away unsteadily and loudly complained, "You shouldn't park in the middle of the street."

I moved to the edge of the lot, stopped, and picked up the map from the passenger seat. I considered sliding south into Nebraska from Pine Ridge. It was less than a five-minute drive, but I was starting to suspect that my leapfrog game had now become avoidance. I went on the road trip knowing it was best for Paula and me to be apart. She agreed.

Together we'd become toxic and hurtful, unable to truly see or hear each other. I was hurt and angry, but also fearful, and running away was what the girl child in me often did when afraid. I needed to hide.

Retreating west was also a way for me to find my mom's roots, researching a family I'd never really known. My grandparents moved east to Sudbury from Heath, Alberta, after my grandfather was unable to keep up the hard labour that kept the homestead going. He had rheumatic fever as a child, which damaged his heart, and he died shortly after moving from a heart attack. He was forty-three.

When we were younger, my brothers and I had only heard about our relatives in the west. In Edmonton, I met a couple of distant cousins, and never good with small talk, we spent an awkward evening having a meal and talking. The discomfort dimmed somewhat when they were topped up with a couple bottles of wine.

I drove away happy and content, abundant with knowledge about the beginnings of my ancestral lines, and I'd gotten answers to questions that created more questions. Albertans are proud of their history, and the resource material had been much more detailed than I'd expected. I was satisfied, but I wasn't yet soft enough in my heart to return home to Paula.

Is my heart softer today? Is hers? I'd say yes. We were texting and talking. There was no sign of the underlayer of resentment and blame that accompanied our early finger-pointing and shaming.

I went back to John's hospitalizations over the years before he died. Paula didn't want to take the time to visit him in the hospital, and when she did, her bitterness lay on her like a heavy wet coat in a storm. It was palpable. Angry, I'd tell her to stay at home. She'd shut down. Angrier, I'd suggest she leave, in many not-so-nice ways.

The night John died, I had a fleeting thought to call Paula; she had been spending some nights with her parents, but I didn't because I knew it would turn into an argument about something. We'd battled over paying for a television for his room, attending meetings with his social worker, buying him clean clothes, looking after his apartment, and paying his bills. Our conflicts were becoming as common as walking the dogs and shovelling snow. Then there was the part of me that wanted to call her because then I'd be able to say, "Look, he's dead. How do you feel now?"

Thoughts of John brought back the sound of his body bag scraping the floor. The attendants couldn't bring the stretcher into his apartment because the hall and door openings were too small. I wanted to see him before they dragged him away, but the attending officer said that it wouldn't be a good idea. A bell I couldn't unring. Craig, Mark, and I did see him later, his bloated face and chest purple with lividity. It was hard, draining, the four of us together for the last time. I wanted to pinch him so that he'd wake up.

I shook my bleak reverie and returned to the map. My plan was to continue east on Highway 18 and veer north at some point towards Wounded Knee and Porcupine. I started the Edge, put her transmission in drive, and slowly rolled out of Big Bat's lot. The swaying man waved; I waved back.

Shrubs and overgrowth had found purchase on fences, sheds, steps, and foundations of buildings in the town proper. Native Stylz, a brightly painted, graffitied barber shop, advertised different cuts, including fades and tapers. Like those of its neighbour, its doors and windows were covered with metal frames, infilled with a heavy steel mesh, and secured by locks.

The SuAnne Big Crow Boys and Girls Club was the most modern building I had seen since visiting the campus at Red Cloud. Its side was graced by a stylized medicine wheel with an image of holding hands in the middle and four feathers dropping from the bottom arc.

A sign near the eastern end of the building announced that the Happy Town Café was now open. Except it wasn't.

SuAnne Big Crow was born and raised on Pine Ridge. A star basketball player, it was her dream to have a "happy town," a place for young people to play, learn, and be safe from drugs, alcohol, violence, and gangs. In 1992, after she died in a car accident, SuAnne's vision was realized, becoming the first charter Boys and Girls Club on a reservation.

Within throwing distance of the café, signs of poverty and insecurity were rife. Houses had empty spaces where there should have been windows. Scraps of salvaged plywood were nailed over some openings, while air conditioners hung haphazardly in others. There were broken doors with missing handles and corners. Children's bicycles leaned against wasted siding or were abandoned among the rusted, bent frames and bodies of cars and trucks dispersed from one yard to the next. Tarps, weighted down with tires, were draped across roofs of trailers. A community disconnected from the economic engine of the American dream.

Despite the impoverishment, there was a stark and wild, natural beauty to the vast landscape. This was a land to be felt and experienced. When I left the gift store at Red Cloud, a poster was advertising a documentary presented by Sinte Gleska University titled *We Are a Horse Nation*. The university was a couple of hours away on the Rosebud Reservation, which abutted the eastern boundaries of Pine Ridge. The Rosebud Sioux Tribe, a branch of the Lakota, are known as the *Sicangu Oyate*, which translates as "Burnt Thigh Nation."

Looking beyond the meagre housing, over the plains disappearing into the horizon, it wasn't hard to imagine the thundering hooves of decorated horses trampling grasses. I saw clouds of rising dust like vortexes, swirling around the determined cries of riders in war paint.

The radio was tuned to *Native America Calling* hosted by Tara Gatewood; her voice accompanied me past fields of sunflowers. The conversation centred around food insecurity, hunger, and lack of nutrition. They discussed how fast food was convenient, less expensive, and easier to ship out to reservations, and how healthy foods were not available or too expensive. Mention was made of traditional culinary practices, and of the fact that Elders were the hardest to serve from community pantries because they didn't want to take food from someone else. They also touched on how Grandmothers and Grandfathers fought the stigma of being poor and needing help. It all sounded too familiar.

* * *

On a sunny morning a week after the DNA results, I met my sister and her husband Guy at their home in a small town outside of Sudbury. Guy was a big man and seemed nervous; sweat had gathered on his brow, and I felt his body heat when we hugged. Denise was waiting at the top of the stairs, and we smiled at each other. It felt right; there wasn't any of the awkwardness I imagined during the drive over from Craig's place in Levack. We got mugs of coffee and settled in at their kitchen table.

It was obvious Denise had spent quite a few hours compiling a set of photographs of Marcus with his family. Her notes accompanying them were written in a beautiful cursive that, oddly enough, reminded me of my mom's writing. She had also taken time to list Marcus's personality traits—he was stubborn, generous, and controlling. He was also a romantic with a good work ethic who loved country music and animals. I wanted to tell her that I too loved old-time country music but thought my early eagerness would be seen as something akin to despairingly needing a connection. And, showing a practical side that came from her time as a personal support worker, she gave me a list of his health issues.

When Denise showed me a picture of Marcus with his mom and dad at their fiftieth wedding anniversary, I finally saw him as a younger man. I could see why my mom would have been attracted to him. He was rugged and handsome and tall. He had a look like my Uncle Daryl—masculine and strong. He looked like a man who worked hard and played hard. I'd talked to Daryl about my mom having an affair with Marcus to see if he knew about it. He was surprised by the news, but offered, "Bev was always attracted to the rough and tough ones."

Denise pushed a side-by-side photo across the table towards me. On one side was a picture of Marcus and his wife on their wedding day in

1948, and on the other was a picture taken on their fiftieth wedding anniversary. "It's amazing. Thank you," I replied.

I appreciated her efforts, taking the time to arrange this picture and printing out all the other photos, but the intimacy of them made me feel uneasy. I believed if I were a stranger, they would have landed better in my gut; instead, they made it churn with apprehension. I tried to hide my discomfort by using enthusiastic exclamations. I kept saying "Wow," "That's amazing," and "Thank you."

My anxiety didn't come from Denise. She was more than I could ever have hoped for. She and Guy were kind, funny, honest, accommodating, and genuinely interested in my life without any taint of judgment. My discomfort came from feeling like I was creeping into Marcus and his family's life. A stalker. It was like I hadn't purchased a ticket, instead slipping through the back door of the theatre.

I was the illegitimate child. I knew I was illegitimate before, but I didn't know what it really felt like until now. I was unable to shake the sense of being a prowler, a voyeur circling a snow globe, allowed to see Marcus but not able to touch, talk, smell, or feel the energy of his presence. And no amount of shaking or rearranging the lineup of photos changed that.

It was also possible my uneasiness was based in the belief that I should have felt something deep and primal for this man who sired me, but I didn't. I had been waiting for a fluttering, a surge, a rising of something, anything at all, but there was nothing. I was feeling flat, uninspired. Smashing the globe against the wall wasn't an option, but I wondered what it would take to work up some emotion.

A couple of hours later, I opened my laptop and took Denise and Guy through a series of pictures my brothers and I had compiled after my mom's passing. We each had a few pictures personally, but most were offered up by our Uncle Ken, Eric's brother.

One was memorable for me. It was taken at Eric's parents' place out on the highway. My mom and I were both getting into the car, and we paused while standing to look at the camera. We were smiling, the similarities obvious in our hair colour, cheeks, chin, nose, and eyes. I had my hand on the handle of the open back door. I was likely six, making my mom twenty-six, very much in her prime. She seemed genuinely happy posing for the photographer, and in line with the fashion of the day she had a bit more than her natural hair curled up and pinned in a bun on top of her head. She was beautiful.

We scrolled through several photos of our family camping and socializing; there were lots of us as kids posing and playing. I offered to email a batch of them to Denise, and she happily accepted.

When it was time to say goodbye, we were all tapped out from six hours of visiting. We hugged, and before leaving, I convinced Denise to take a selfie. While we are the same height, we couldn't be more opposite in appearance. Denise had blondish light hair, fuzzy and curly, pulled back and up, and I had dark hair, short and layered. She was wearing large chrome earrings and a girlish turquoise-and-black top, and she somehow managed to do a raised-eyebrow pose behind modern tortoise-framed glasses. I had a close-mouthed grin and was wearing faded plaid and worn jeans.

I didn't believe we'd be ever mistaken by a stranger for being sisters despite the similarities in our cheeks and chins, and possibly our noses. That was fine with me because what was most important was that we recognized each other for who we were. We were Marcus's daughters.

* * *

I hesitated to make this story longer, but I needed to let you know I changed the names of my father and his family to protect their identity. It was not my preferred choice. Friends have put it to me that we all had choices, and while I agreed I could have made a different one, in this request, I deferred to my older sister.

Marcus's wife is still alive, and my father's family wanted to keep the news of my existence from reaching her. I understood. She is over ninety years old and had spent a long, at times difficult, life raising a family and living with a man who required a significant amount of care before he passed. She deserved to spend the rest of her life in grace and peace.

It has been five years since I surfaced, and I am very grateful for finding Denise. We have called each other frequently and visited occasionally. I have socialized with my niece and nephew and met a couple of their kids. I feel like I have been taken care of by her and

Guy. And keeping the family's identity private was the right decision for me. Besides, it was not mine to give. I have left it up to them to claim this story.

I never heard anything more from my sister who sent the original DNA request. This made me sad, but considering the circumstances of our births, I completely understood her position. We were the same age. Her mom was seven months pregnant with her when I was conceived. I couldn't say I understood her feelings about this because I didn't know them, but I do know something about having your life turned upside down, feeling betrayed, and having questions where there will never be any answers.

I was more than satisfied to have found the answer to my big question and to have written the ending to my mom's story. Through overcoming fears and reaching out, I discovered all my true relations. I was happy and settled, even though I had gone from being one family's secret to another family's secret. It was ironic, and in my earlier life, I might have felt resentment, but I wasn't upset. I was offered what I needed from a sister with a big, loving heart. What more was there?

CHAPTER 14
I'M STILL COUNTING

STICKING TO MY PLAN, I travelled east from Pine Ridge and north through Wounded Knee. I learned that this was where, in late December of 1890, Chief Big Foot (Spotted Elk) surrendered to army forces. He was killed in the ensuing massacre, which was triggered by a gunshot while soldiers were confiscating weapons. Survivors told stories of a Hotchkiss machine gun cutting down women and children, and of how Spotted Elk, ill with pneumonia, was killed where he lay. There was a tragic photo of him lying dead in the snow. Depending on the report, between 20 and 25 soldiers and 150 Sioux were killed, half of them women and children. Other historians put the number as twice that.

The reservation roads were essentially lengthy paved trails between small towns that dotted the plains. Signage was scarce, and shoulders, if present, were narrow, slippery-looking slices of sand.

It was early afternoon when I entered the northern Badlands through the Ben Reifel Visitor Center. Shelves held dozens of books about Crazy Horse, Sitting Bull, and Red Cloud, among other lesser-known people.

I learned the Badlands were first formed by sediment deposits such as ash, sand, silt, clay, and fossil soils shaped by wind and water. Half a million years ago, the erosion started when the Cheyenne River captured the waters from the Black Hills, carving fantastic shapes into what had been flat floodplains.

The spires and pinnacles of the Badlands were testaments to the sediment layers, and scientists suggested that with an erosion rate of one inch per year, the Badlands will cease to exist in a half million years.

I guess this is the time to visit then, instead of getting lunch, complained Fat Chick.

I steered the Edge onto the paved circuit to take in the sights. At the pullovers, I saw plates on vehicles from South Carolina, New Jersey, New York, and Alberta. One had a sticker that proudly proclaimed they stopped for turtles, and another stated we should all live kindly and simply. Signs also cautioned visitors to be aware of rattlesnakes.

My ride through the Badlands became a series of jumping from one pullover to the next. The landscape was otherworldly, and being in it, absorbed and surrounded—as opposed to driving by it on Pine Ridge—was unlike anything I had ever experienced.

The sediment layers of soft pastels—bands of reds, yellows, and browns shaped into mounds and spires and pinnacles by natural abrasion—showed how the energy of earth had created itself. The land called to me in a venerable spiritual tone. I heard it when the wind whispered around the abutments, moving through the grasses. The grasslands, foliage, and wildflowers were the final touches of an earthly creation.

I met a herd of bighorn sheep crossing the pavement, and soon after, the barking calls of prairie dogs popping in and out of their burrows filled the air. It was warm enough to be dressed in shorts and a t-shirt. There were a few tourists around, and I gradually got into a rhythm with one couple I kept seeing over and over.

Driving a Jeep Grand Cherokee, they pulled in seconds after me at one lookout area. We were alone in the parking lot and got out of our cars at the same time.

"Lock the doors," the woman barked to her partner as she walked towards the lookout.

"What? I'm right here."

She turned back. "Lock. The. Doors."

The man looked over at me in sympathy, and like the snap of a rifle shot, I heard the locks of their Jeep engage.

At the lookout, there were sheep on the ledges beneath us—it seemed like an impossible descent for them to have made. I risked a glance at the couple. He was tall, fit-looking, and sandy-haired with a kind face.

I remarked, "It's incredible how surefooted they are."

He nodded. "It is impressive."

She was more difficult to read because she wouldn't look at me. Her hair was black and wrapped up in a bun that sat more on the back of her head than the top. A kind of white doily thing kept it all together. Skinny Bitch showed up. *Fuck her and her hefty ass, skin blemishes, and moustache. How about we rip that doily thing off her head and run? I could take her.* But I couldn't.

I left them at the railing and walked back to the Edge, grinning at how I would have looked: hiking double-time down the road in my spongy crocs, a doily clutched in one hand while the other was holding my boobs to stop them from trampling my face.

I exited the park and headed towards the town of Wall.

* * *

George's legs encircled the chair I was sitting in. His right knee pressed into my thigh, his belly and chest pushed against my side. The heat of George's body was welcome, and when he turned away to pick up more ink, I got a chill, like a warm blanket had been lifted in the early morning. It wasn't chilly in his shop, but I was cold anyway. It seemed to be an enduring state now that I was almost sixty years old.

We were the only people in his space, four or five steps below street level on Kingston's Ontario Street. Bare stone and brick walls provided backdrops for hanging skateboards; pieces of contemporary art, framed and unframed; and mirrors.

The half walls of the shop counters were covered with simple black wooden frames holding sheets of flash art. Against the walls, benches made from an assembly of reclaimed timber and cast-iron pipefittings sat, ready for customers.

A room off to the left, at the bottom of the stairs, was fitted with a bar counter at one end. The rest of the space was taken up with lights, microphones, and big box speakers. George and his pals used it when visiting musician friends wanted to party.

George's left hand, gloved in black latex, pushed into the top of my shoulder, right at the base of my neck. His other hand, also gloved, held a tattoo machine. George was inking an old-school rose on my neck using thick lines and bright colours. Several years ago, while working out of an uptown shop, he tattooed an anchor with a rope and banner with the word TRUTH on the back of my hand.

When he pivoted on his stool to pick up some more ink from his bench, I straightened my neck to stretch out the muscles. They couldn't help but scream and tighten against his assault. It was a welcome violation though. The tattoo was my gift to myself for my fifty-ninth birthday.

George gave me time to stretch and twist before I went back to supporting my head with my left hand. I anchored my elbow firmly to the arm of the chair, and bared my neck, like a puppy would towards an alpha looking to dominate. He rolled towards me, clutched my body again with his, and continued his work.

My armpits were dark with sweat. I sniffed them out, trying to smell anything other than shop disinfectant and the gel that George had used to slick back his hair. I stopped shaving my body hair years ago. After trying to smear deodorant onto straggles of armpit hair that looked gross and frankly felt meaningless, I had quit that practice as well, choosing to live with whatever odours my body secretes.

My mom, if she were still alive, would be disappointed in me. Not because I was lacking in personal hygiene—although it was possible this could cause her some chagrin as well—but more because I'd covered her tattooed face on my leg with hair, and lots of it. I did at one time use her portrait as a reason to shave my legs, and after letting the burden of hair removal build up more angst in our relationship, I said the hell with it and let her face become furry. I decided that if I ever broke my sobriety, I'd shave around her portrait in one of my many drunken stupors, leaving enough hair to create a beard for her. In my deluded mind, we'd laugh drunkenly while toasting each other's lives.

George's breath, hot on my neck, ceased its steady rhythm as he started another section of the outline near my jaw. It stung like a dozen relentless little pinches into the soft flesh on the back of your arm. *Fuuuuck, that hurts.* I wanted to slap him. He wiped my neck roughly with a folded paper towel that he held between two fingers of his left hand. Over the hour, we worked steadily through a routine of grasping, holding, inking, clenching, wiping, pivoting, washing, and stretching. We got through the outline, then the black shading. We were finally into the laying in of colours. *Hallelujah with an amen.*

Near the end of applying the colour, George's continuous wiping of ink and blood had become more painful than the needlework. The wiping pulled at my skin, aggravating it, and I was getting pissed with him, way past the slapping stage. I found myself clenching my fists and tightening my jaw. *What the fuck dude, why wipe three times when once will do? Like seriously.*

I'd have never said anything out loud because I wanted him at his best. I had come across fragile artists who either collapsed at any perceived criticism of their art or went off the rails and refused to finish inking the offender who dared to complain. Not that George's confidence would have collapsed on me if I mentioned his rough wiping—he seemed more like a guy who'd have difficulty staying on track after an infraction, gradually getting more and more pissed before losing his mind in a big way. Besides, I was getting exactly what I came looking for: pain with a side of colour. If there was anyone to blame, I should look in the mirror.

With some finishing touches left, I asked, "Are you pleased?"

"Yeah, it's awesome. I love doing necks because they're so visible."

* * *

It didn't escape me that I belonged to a generation where most people disapproved of tattoos. Regardless, I was still collecting. Before inking my hand and neck, I could always cover my tattoos. That way, I exposed myself only to those who I thought were going to be respectful. I had no control over how my skin art was seen by others, but I heard the comments: *Why would you do that to yourself? Are you going to beat me up? What are you going to do when you get old? You know you can't wash that off.*

I didn't answer them because there wasn't any understanding in the asking.

Now, it wasn't possible to hide my collection. I didn't want to be invisible anymore. I wanted others to know this was who I am. I existed, and I had always been this person. I found my relevance by working through childhood issues of domestication, all the rules about what I should look like, how I should behave, and what roles I needed to be good at to be loved and accepted by family and society.

With the sloughing off of the judgment, labels and expectations, my confidence bloomed. I was far removed from the girl my mom imagined and hoped I would become. I wished she were alive so I could meet her.

While I may have confidence in who I was, I still experienced stigma and stereotyping. A couple of days before meeting up with George, I was leaving the washroom at Walmart when I met an older woman accompanied by a young child coming in. "Mon dieu," she exclaimed before turning to see if she was in the right washroom. I stopped. When she looked back, I found her eyes and said, "it's okay, you're in the right place."

Paula was outside waiting for me. She would have come in like she usually does to, in her words, run interference and give people who stare at me her own impression of the evil eye, but she was at customer service. "Did you see her?" I asked.

"Yeah, sorry you had to experience that."

"It's okay. I'm better at handling their stuff than I used to be." I breathed in deeply, continuing, "before I'd let it ruin my day. I know I can't control how people identify me. What they see through their filters and experience is what they perceive. If it's a man, that's okay. If it's something else, then that's okay too, but it's frustrating. And it still happens no matter how far out I stick my tits." I took another deep breath, "and I'm even wearing brightly coloured, girlie leggings." I kick out my leg to emphasize the turquoise and white leggings Paula had picked up for me, "I guess I need pink flowers and unicorns on my next pair." We laughed and held hands as we made our way through the stacks to the pharmacy section.

The stigmas and stereotyping also came from professionals. Four years previous, in 2015, I went to see Dr. Jack, a dermatologist, because I was having problems with skin fragility on the backs of my hands. Paula and I were waiting in the consultation room, and we could hear most of his conversation next door with another patient.

When we got seated in the exam room, he rolled over in his chair to hold my hands, looking over the top of them. Within seconds of seeing them, he told me, "You have porphyria."

"Okay, what's that?"

"PCT or Porphyria Cutanea Tarda. It's usually caused by Hepatitis C. Have you ever been an intravenous drug user?"

I looked sideways at Paula. *What the fuck?* "No."

"Do you have a liver doctor?"

"No."

"Do you drink?"

"No."

"Are you sure?"

"Yeah, I'm sure. I've been sober for thirteen years."

"It must be the tattoos then."

Every question Dr. Jack asked me was loud and abrupt. I suspected he had some hearing loss. He didn't seem to believe me when I told him I hadn't used drugs, I didn't drink, and that, while I hadn't insisted on new needles with every tattoo, I had always visited reputable shops, never a scratcher.

"Yup, it's probably the tattoos. We'll get you tested for Hep C."

After I asked him to write down the diagnosis, he said, "Give us a week or so, and then you can call in for the results."

For the next week, I was crazy with worry about possibly having Hepatitis C, a disease known to lay dormant and then strike my cohort in their later years. It's a virus contracted from partying, poor choices, and uninhibited and unprotected sex. Sounded like my young life. I googled it every day, looking for causes, conditions, treatments, good outcomes, and poor ones. It wasn't a good idea.

I called in for the results early.

"I'm sorry Dr. Jack is in with a patient."

"Can you please ask him if you can tell me my results?" I tried to sit, but I was unable to, so I walked back and forth for a minute or more before the receptionist came back on the phone. "You're negative for Hep C."

I collapsed into a chair, smiled, and let out the long breath I felt like I had been holding for a week.

Dr. Jack referred me to Dr. Bratt at the Civic Hospital because part of the treatment for PCT was a phlebotomy. I imagined some underground chamber where I would be laid out on a stone plinth, my arms hanging over the sides, while blood dripping from cuts sliced along my wrists was collected in gutters carved out of the granite floor.

Dr. Bratt's intern called my name, and when I got up, she looked past me towards Paula. She was confused and embarrassed when I told her I was the Lorrie Potvin she called. Paula came with me, we joked a bit, and together, we got her through the preliminary questions about allergies, drugs, onset, and timing.

Dr. Bratt came in and confirmed the diagnosis.

"I'm going to send you for testing for all the Hepatitis viruses."

"But I'm negative."

"I'd like to confirm." Head down, she shuffled through the intern's notes. After a moment, she asked, "So… you don't drink?"

"No."

"Not even a little wine on Saturday?" She mimed drinking out of an imaginary glass.

I could feel my face heating up. *Is she for fucking real?* I didn't look towards Paula because I was afraid I'd say it out loud. "No, I'm sober."

"Ooooookay." She drew the word out in a way that implied skepticism. "Soooooo you're not taking any hormones?"

"No. I used to take hormone replacement during menopause, but not for a while now."

"No hormones at all?" she tried again.

"No."

"So, you did take hormones, but no hormones now?"

I twisted towards Paula with a questioning look. *What the hell is this?* As soon as I said it in my mind, I made the connection. "No, I'm not transitioning or taking testosterone."

"Well, I had to ask."

Are you serious?

After the blood tests, collecting my urine for twenty-four hours, and being bled three times over a month in the day clinic, my Porphyria was under control. There was no definitive cause or cure in my case. Dr. Bratt advised me to avoid any trauma, like getting more tattoos, because of my tendency towards skin fragility. She also told me not to take any ibuprofen, to avoid the sun, to always wear sunscreen, and not to drink.

* * *

George peeled back his gloves, dropped them into a garbage can, and stood up to stretch. His white t-shirt looked like it had been freshly pressed and was in keeping with his barbered look and trimmed black beard.

We looked at my new piece in a mirror, and we were both pleased. He wrapped my neck with a bandage and explained the aftercare schedule.

I counted out cash and added on forty dollars as a tip. "Thanks again, George. I love it, man. I'll be back."

EPILOGUE

THE ROAD HOME

THE WALMART SUPERCENTRE IN PIERRE, South Dakota, was my host for the night. I rolled in a few minutes shy of nine o'clock and was very happy for the rest from driving the plains. Flat and rolling for miles on miles, vacant of trees with a few exceptions around the river channels, the land was mesmerizing and draining.

Before leaving Wall, I visited the famous Wall Drug Store. It was a stimulating complex that sold art, western wear, leather goods, camping gear, clothes, trinkets, souvenirs, and jewellery. It even contained a chapel, a café, and an apothecary museum complete with flocks of stuffed birds, mounted heads, and other critters. There were possibly a million other things I may have missed—no exaggerating.

Amusingly, I ran into doily lady looking at trinkets. I walked around to her left and stopped to look at some sunglasses. I sensed she knew I was there. I looked at her, waiting for longer than I normally would, but she still wouldn't acknowledge me, no eye contact. Instead of taking the natural way, like you would if you were browsing, she backed up, twisting away among the displays, and disappeared. *Maybe we need lunch*, suggested Fat Chick.

Around eight o'clock the next morning, I drove over to the Pierre Aquatic Centre. "Hi, I'm from out of town. I'm wondering if I could take a shower. Or should I come back and pay for a public swim?" I was hoping the woman behind the counter would say it was fine for me to take a shower since the public swim wasn't until ten o'clock. I wanted to get on the road, and I wasn't very keen on changing and showering with a throng of people.

She looked up from the chair she was sitting in and hesitated—like she wanted to come around the counter to have a full look at me—before answering. I slipped my right hand, the back of which was fully tattooed, into the pocket of my hoodie and tried to smile an "aren't we like best friends?" smile. I waited.

"We'll let you take a shower. Come on, and I'll show you." She was a tall woman, and her long strides led me through several doors, down a floor, around a corner or two, and into a large locker room and change area. There were several showers accessed through a wide opening in the block wall.

"Thank you so much. I won't be long."

The hot water was a gift, and I spent more time than usual standing in the steam, easing a few of the aches that came with sleeping in a car. It was bliss, and even though I heard voices in the locker room area, I didn't encounter another person. Fat Chick was grateful.

* * *

At home, I would go swimming at the Plant, a facility near where Paula and I lived. It had a steam room. My routine was to get warm in the room, then swim my laps, finishing with another stint in the steam. It worked for me, but the facility was popular and could be quite crowded. What didn't work were the stares when I undressed and showered in the women's change room.

Tattoos cover my chest and arms, and I've had women shake their heads while staring at me. Others, startled by me joining them in the communal showers, have turned off their shower and left, forgetting the shampoo bubbles still in their hair. The most common response came from those who stared, all the while trying not to.

I do have to say that children were the best. Once a small girl, newly post-toddler, her towel dragging over the wet floor, shyly came over to the bench where I was sitting, drying my legs. She pointed at my arm, her eyes bright and curious, touched one of my tattoos with her little forefinger. "What that?"

Her mom who had been distracted, suddenly noticed she had come over to me. "Omigosh, I'm so sorry. Sara, come over here, honey."

I smiled reassuringly. "No worries. It's all good." I held my arm out to show her an old-school dove on my right arm. It had a ribbon in its beak that was weaved through two hearts. The ribbon was inscribed with the date Paula and I got married. "They are pictures that tell the story of my life." I smiled at mom and then back to Sara, "are we good?" She nodded like she'd been given a great secret to hold, and then toddled quickly back to her mom in the stick-legged, stomping style of those still seeking their natural rhythm.

* * *

I got lost leaving the change room, but another woman, holding some papers and a folder, saw me looking around corners trying to find my way out and offered to walk me up to the front desk. I thanked her, waved at the women behind the glass, and walked out to the Edge, feeling very grateful, clean, and invigorated, and cared for by generous and good people.

Heading north, I passed through Selby and turned west towards Mobridge on Highway 12. Before traversing the bridge over Lake Oahe, I was greeted by three church billboards in a row. The devotion to Christ chimed in with "protect the unborn" messages. Nothing much happens in the colonized world that didn't have a purpose, so I wondered what the intention was for their placement as the highway only led, in that direction, to the Standing Rock Reservation.

My natural skepticism of authority made it difficult for me to be objective about the church because of its past complicity in attempting to solve the "Indian problem." Were these billboards another modern-day attempt?

Lake Oahe was a reservoir named after the 1874 Oahe Indian Mission. Started in the '30s and finished by the '60s, the Army Corps of Engineers built five dams on the Missouri River, forcing large populations of pioneers and Native Americans to relocate. Over 200,000 acres on the Cheyenne River Reservation and the Standing Rock Reservation were flooded, displacing a village, and ejecting one third of Standing Rock's tribal membership to higher grounds, land that was flat and dry but offering little protection from the harsher elements.

To generate power and build irrigation canals, the Corps devastated the landscape. The fertile bottomlands were lost, forests were destroyed, and sacred spaces and burial grounds were submerged, lost forever. And now the Corps was back to show its support of the Dakota Access Pipeline (DAPL), which would cross the Standing Rock Reservation and pass under Lake Oahe uninhibited.

Sacred Stone Camp, the protest site, was organized in the spring to bring attention to the DAPL's threat to the area's clean water and to the infringement of the pipeline on burial grounds. The news told me the encampment was located on the Cannonball River, where it meandered along the lowlands before joining the Missouri. I headed north on Road 1806. I was nervous.

The camp appeared in a field by the river. There were flags, teepees, tents, motorhomes, corrals, cars, trucks. And men in a hut at the entrance. My stomach got tight, and I tussled with a very strong urge to drive right by. *I can do this. I want to do this.* I slowed and turned right.

A wiry man wearing jeans and a t-shirt, with a red bandana circling his brown forehead and black hair, came up to my window. "Are you camping or visiting?"

There was no request for a secret password or a special handshake, and he didn't ask me any questions about my motives, tribal affiliation, or ancestry. "I'm camping for a couple of days."

"Wait until we smudge your car, then go straight in." Another man, in similar dress, joined him, and they walked around the Edge, swinging steel paint cans that had handles fashioned out of steel coat hangers, fanning smoke from burning cedar over my car. I found out later the men belonged to the Red Warrior Society camp of water protectors.

I drove down the hill into camp slowly. It was just after four o'clock in the afternoon. The sun had been with me all day. I appreciated its illumination now as I crawled my way through the stands of brightly coloured tribal flags flanking the roads. Multi-coloured messages of love and hope had been scrawled on a teepee cover laid flat on the grass alongside the dirt track.

I easily recognized a few flags belonging to the Mohawk, Seminole, Iroquois, and United Sioux Nations. There were even Canadian and pride flags displayed along the main entrance route.

Surrounded by hundreds of people, possibly thousands, the space felt much like the time I went to a popular local country fair with its colourful attractions and rides, open spaces, and clusters of visitors.

Some people were sitting under temporary shelters made of blue tarps held up by posts and ropes, others were walking in groups or gathered around fires, and still more seemed to be organizing their camps. One man, with long stringy brown hair hanging from a dark ball cap, was sitting on a bicycle, catching a ride through camp by clenching a flagpole tied to the side of a late model Nissan Pathfinder.

The Nissan was leaving the camp, its roof rack loaded with storage bins, tarps, tents, and collapsible tables and chairs. Red gas cans were strapped to its side, and a collection of youth fringe culture stickers and logos plastered the back window and tailgate.

I drove through the camp along the river, passing clusters of portable toilets and motorhomes, before deciding to back into a space at the bottom of a grass-covered rise near the highway. All my apprehension had melted away, and I felt like the camp was exactly where I needed to be. Here, I could be part of something much bigger than myself. I felt privileged and honoured.

I was unpacking and organizing my gear and mulling over the pros and cons of putting up my tent when I heard the unmistakable sound of a Harley. A man pulled into the space beside me. His ride was a fairly new Softail, customized with ape hangers, front and rear crash bars, studded leather bags, and a windshield covered with bugs and scratches. I assumed he belonged to the small, orange, one-person tent that was set up a few yards away.

He killed the engine, kicked out his jiffy stand, and started to untie pieces of wood that had been secured to his back seat. I went over to help and introduced myself.

The man told me his name was Ely and shook my hand enthusiastically. We dropped the wood near a small fire pit beside his tent. Dressed completely in black, Ely was a Navajo man in his senior years. He was wearing biker boots, elastic bands around the legs of his pants (which seemed more suited for bicycling to the office than riding the road), and a black leather jacket with a matching leather ball cap. A sparse moustache sat on his upper lip.

He thanked me, and I returned to the Edge, rearranged my cooler, and unfolded my chair. I decided not to set up my tent as it was supposed to rain the next couple of days. It would be drier and warmer in the car.

The community kitchen and gathering area were the hub of the camp. It was a sprawling campus of tables and temporary structures thrown together and covered in green, black, and blue tarps. A mix of folding chairs surrounded a sacred fire in the centre of a large open space that had been trampled down to dirt.

To one side of the open space, abutting the camp kitchen, were large community cooking fires with grills. A coffee crew rotated huge percolators on and off the heat, continually dumping and refilling them to keep a row of large dispensers, the size of highway construction cones, filled with hot coffee.

Water containers of various sizes, either on wheels or trailers, were lined up near a smoker barbeque rig the size of a small oil tanker truck. It was rusty and blackened with smoke. The kitchen roof itself was held up by racks of shelves and posts tied to tables where food was laid out three times a day by volunteers.

Handy stacks of split wood were piled close to all the fires, and a temporary fence sectioned off the space that was being used for the bulk of firewood. I arrived in time to join a line and helped unload wood from a transport truck.

After unloading, I sat on a bench under a shelter near the sacred fire. I made eye contact with a young woman with shoulder-length blonde hair and blue eyes. We acknowledged the other with slight nods and introduced ourselves. Her name was Sarah.

"Where are you from?" she asked.

"Ottawa, Ontario."

"Whaaaat? That's great!" She said excitedly, and then continued without taking a breath: "I'm from South Carolina."

A small woman in her thirties, Sarah had been at the camp for over a week; she said she was going to head home in a week or so. "When the spirit moves," she smiled. She told me her family name was Robicheaux, and then shared a few stories about her clan's celebrations, which occurred twice a year and were dedicated to celebrating their Métis heritage.

I thought back to my mom getting drunk and blaming "the Indian in me." Being Métis is something I related to, but I wouldn't say it out loud. I knew who I was on my mom's side, and there was no native blood in the Potvin line as far as I could discern. I wasn't really expecting to find any. Craig once asked our uncle about Indigenous roots, and Daryl's negative response was so vehement that he practically burst a vein.

I was reminded of the quote from Sir John A. Macdonald, Canada's first prime minister, about taking "the Indian out of the child." My cohort was not far removed from the days when Indigenous people were herded onto reserves and into residential schools or taken away to be adopted by white people in the Sixties Scoop.

The early policy of assimilation, today called cultural genocide, forced those who were Indigenous to hide their identities and shun their ancestry to safely join the dominant culture. They denied being Indigenous because they didn't want to go to reserves. They wanted to live free on their own land without being numbered like cattle, with an Indian Agent controlling their existence and a church insisting on their attendance.

Now that the truth was unfolding, the threads of colonization were unravelling, and nation-to-nation reconciliation and reparations will take decades, possibly more, to make closer to right.

I asked Sarah about some of the activities in the camp, and she told me about a water walk she went on a few days previous in the city of Bismarck.

The participants were coached by the leaders and Elders to walk in peace, softly and slowly, on the sidewalks only. They were adamantly told not to use foul language or violence, or to exhibit any form of aggression. They were also directed not to walk on the road or to disrupt traffic in any way because they'd be exposed to arrest.

Unlike the Red Warrior Society, who believed in protest and resistance marches led by their leaders on horseback and often took more aggressive forms of direct action, the water protectors wanted to send the message that they were not protestors, but the peaceful protectors of sacred water. Water meant life, and it was their duty as caretakers to pray for the water, to assemble in a non-violent way, and to walk for the preciousness of all life.

We were interrupted when a brown woman walked past, her long black hair swung in a braid down her back. She was carrying a large bag of loose tobacco. She stopped and offered me a large pinch. "Thank you for coming," she said.

I took it in my left hand and responded, "Meegweetch," which meant *thank you* in Anishinaabemowin. When she moved on, I realized she hadn't offered Sarah any. *Is it because I have brown eyes and dark hair?* Sarah looked away and didn't acknowledge the slight. I said a quick prayer and dusted the tobacco off my palm into the sacred fire.

The call for the evening meal was made by Ian, a tall, large-bellied man with a booming voice. He used a microphone from a temporary shelter tacked on to the side of the administrative tent to let people know the elders, the grandmothers and grandfathers, would be fed first.

Soon after his announcement, a slender young woman carrying a large tote filled with stacks of plates covered with aluminum foil made her way towards us. She put the tote down in front of me and asked if I wanted dinner.

Surprised, I put up my hand to stop her. "No, no, I'm okay. Thank you."

"Here, please take one."

I felt my face getting red. "No, no, it's all good. I'll get in line."

"Are you sure?" Doubt clouded her features.

"Yes, thanks. I'll be fine."

After another moment of hesitation, with a look that said she really wanted to do her job by dropping a plate in my lap, she skipped Sarah and moved on to a group of men and women beside us.

I didn't know whether to be pleased or not. *Do I look that old?* Damn, I guess I do. Certain communities considered anyone over the age of fifty-two as "technically" an elder or an older person, and I was fifty-seven.

I watched the young people delivering the meals to grandmothers and grandfathers sitting in clusters under the shelters that circled the border of the common area. It was very affirming to see the respect and appreciation for those older ones in the community. Among them would be the Elders, their wisdom earned from a lifetime of creating, storytelling, doing, and being, who were crucial to the continued resurgence of Indigenous Nations and cultures across North America.

Plates were perched on laps, and chatter diminished as people ate. Unlike the parties or get-togethers I attended as an adult—or was excluded from because I was too young—Indigenous gatherings, ceremonies, and feasts would be incomplete without all the community members present, including babies, children, adults, and old people. Sitting among the Elders, grandmothers and grandfathers, at Standing Rock was a humbling that felt right. I belonged.

The mid-September dusk arrived shortly after eight o'clock, and with it, shaded by wisps of clouds, was a full moon. The shining presence of Grandmother Moon was serendipitous. She offered several teachings, mostly about water, because of her influence on the tides and the fertility of women.

I had attended Moon Ceremonies where the group spent the evening hours singing, drumming, laughing, sharing teachings and prayers for a better life in a healing circle, and feasting on a potluck meal before hugging the others goodbye.

Those sharing circles and ceremonies, like the sweat lodge, were where I felt truly accepted and began to heal my feminine spirit for the first time. It was important to recognize my femininity, which I had denied for most of my life, so I could heal the little girl that had been abused and cast aside.

At the same time, it was essential I recognized how strongly I carried the masculine spirit and acknowledged the shame and harm I'd done to myself in trying to hide my true nature. While I didn't pop out of the womb tattooed, I am more the true person I was born today because of being welcomed into healing circles and ceremonies. They helped me shed the burden of my own domestication.

Drummers were starting to assemble around a big drum. I felt like I had found the road home when the drumming started, and the beats began to sound in time with my own heart. A crowd gathered, and soon after one song finished, a round dance started, led by Ian. An eagle feather was pinned to his ball cap, and he held a painted stick with ribbons hanging from it. He guided a line of people behind him, all holding hands and side-stepping while rotating their hands in time with the beat. Jingles joined the drums, and I heard yelping above the high falsettos of the drummers.

Dancers from all nations and colours—black, brown, yellow, red, and white—weaved and undulated around the drums. It was a medley of men and women, young and old, and a few children, all of whom were holding hands, dancing, smiling, and laughing. There was a break in the line; an older man with long white hair stepped in and offered his hand to a younger man dressed in a leather vest, jeans, and boots. He took it with a smile.

This was the part of Standing Rock that wasn't on the news: the joy, the dancing, the laughing, and the love that came from being together as community. The mainstream media seemed to prefer the images of defiance from the confrontations between the Warriors and the oil workers. They streamed the aggressive actions on their news feeds, not the drumming, singing, and praying. They didn't feature the holding of hands, one person connecting with another and then another, a moving expression of humanity.

Most of the Elders I learned from shared the importance of inclusivity as the path to healing, not only for ourselves, but also for our communities and, ultimately, our nations. Everyone was welcome in ceremony, regardless of their race or culture, if they respected each other, helped when and where they could, and followed the ceremonial protocols. To exclude one was not inclusion.

I sat and watched, happily absorbing the vibrations of the drums and the shuffling of feet. The evening had gotten cold; most people had donned jackets, and a few had draped blankets over their shoulders. The dancers faded out one by one. I had gotten up early, and my tired body felt the chill. I reluctantly left the circle to find some warmth.

When I got back to the Edge, Ely was sitting at his fire. He invited me to join him. I brought over my chair and huddled up to the heat.

Ely talked about his career in the railroad after his service in the army, but mostly he told me about his passion: photography. He had brought a small camera with him, but he wished he'd been able to pack more gear into his side bags.

His voice got melancholy and lonely when he told me that his wife back home had found someone else. "We still live together. I love her, but I understand." He poked the fire and continued, "it's been hard, and I needed to come back here."

I learned this was Ely's second trip to the camp from New Mexico. "Were you on your bike for both trips?"

"Yeah, this time was the hardest. I spent two nights on the road. First night I slept in my sleeping bag in a park. The second night I was so tired I slept under a picnic table. I didn't bother taking off my helmet or getting my bag, and when I woke up, there was frost on my jacket."

I knew that kind of tiredness and was impressed with Ely's commitment. He was determined to come back to support the protectors, even though he also needed to distance himself from his wife. I was more impressed when I found out he was sixty-eight years old. I wished I had his stamina, but I couldn't keep my eyes open. The fire was warm, but my back was cold, and I yearned for my sleeping bag and blanket.

"I'll see you in the morning." I picked up my chair.

He stirred the fire. "Yeah."

It rained throughout the night, and the morning brought muted skies, grey and heavy with precipitation yet to fall. The main tracks through the camp were turning into mud.

Ely poked his head out of his tent just as I sat down at my cooler and broke open a boiled egg for breakfast. I had already been to the common kitchen to fill up my thermos with coffee.

"Hey, how you doing? Did you have a good sleep?" I asked.

He grunted an affirmation I couldn't translate and disappeared towards the row of portable toilets near the veterans' camp. He returned with a mug of coffee, sat beside the fire pit, and stirred up the coals. None were hot enough to start a morning fire.

I went over and offered him an egg from the half dozen I boiled up earlier.

He grinned. "Thanks. I love eggs," he said, and then started the task of breaking open the shell. It disappeared quickly, so I offered another. He took it sheepishly.

After breakfast, I walked around to explore the parts of the camp I'd been unable to see the day before. The Chief's section had a long, enclosed, tent-like structure made of canvas, strung between two teepees, like the tents used at outdoor weddings. Its anchor ropes were tied to large wooden spikes driven in the ground.

In the adjacent clearing was a sacred fire circled by stones. A firekeeper was sitting in a small three-sided tent to one side, a stack of logs beside him. He was asleep.

A few tents away, I came upon a group of six women. None seemed to be older than twenty-five or thirty. They told me the group met every morning to pray and sing for the water as they walked through camp down to the river. They asked me if I knew a song to share.

I volunteered, "I know a water song: 'Nibi Wabo.'" I sang part of it for them, and they all started smiling and got excited because it was the same song they had heard the day before. I was happy it was discernable to them because singing was not something I did well.

I was taught that one round of the song was to be sung in each of the four directions. I sang a round for them again—nobody fainted or was offended by my wavering notes—we then faced east to start the song, and when we finished in the north, the group started walking towards the river, still singing.

I abandoned the women as soon as they started taking off their socks and shoes to sink up to their knees into the muddy sides and bottom of the Cannonball River. I didn't have enough faith that I would be able to get myself out of the muck without a crane or a pickup with a winch, so I passed and wished them the best.

I saw a sweat lodge in a clearing by the river. The sweats so far had only been offered to the men as there were no lodgekeepers in the camp that could offer a sweat to the women. I thought about how amazing it would be to participate in a sweat lodge ceremony while at Standing Rock.

After my tour, I stood on Facebook Hill—so named because it was the only place where people could get any reliable cell service—and looked over the whole camp. Just below the hill were two corrals, one of which was occupied by three horses eating from rolls of hay. A couple more horses were grazing freely, and beyond them, smoke plumes rose from fires scattered through camp.

Right at the top of the hill was a white Chrysler ProMaster van. Beside it was an antenna on a sturdy pole. A sign on the van showed it was home to Spirit Resistance Radio on Channel 87.9. A tent was set up behind the van, and while there was a table with what looked like lunch on it, no one was around.

Another sign partway up the hill asked campers not to pitch tents or camp beyond that point so that everyone could come to sit and enjoy the view. It was spectacular, a wonder. I sensed I was part of something big, like I belonged to an energy that defied definition. It was at that moment I understood I was part of the larger question, one to be lived in without any need to seek answers. To always do my best in a good way.

I sat down on the grass and twisted the *mala* around my wrist. It was a parting gift from Paula. The blue tassel was stained from being accidentally dipped into my coffee cup. The shower in Pierre was unable to restore its vibrancy; I hoped this wasn't a sign of the future of our relationship. We hadn't been in touch for a few days. I had been away from home for more than three weeks, and I missed her deeply.

I twisted the *mala* round and round, a circular exercise, thinking to myself, *she loves me, she loves me not.*

I texted her: *At Standing Rock. It's amazing!*

Within seconds, she responded: *Are you safe?*

All good.

Are you coming home soon?

Does she want to see me? Or does she need more time? Has she made a decision? Has something else happened? I stalled, tears started, and a slight tremor twisted my belly.

Are you missing me? I asked her. The shiver flared up into my chest, and I inhaled deeply, my breaths became shorter.

Yes. I love you, she said. And then, *Come home.*

Tears watered my cheeks. I jammed my phone into the front pocket of my shorts and looked over the camp towards the river. I wanted to whoop and yell out across the fields that she loved me and wanted me to come home. I would have left then, but I was over 2,200 kilometres from home, a three-day drive.

I met up with Sarah by chance at the community kitchen around lunch. We joined the lineup and picked up sandwiches and bowls of homemade vegetable soup. The hot soup was welcome on the damp, rainy day.

We were finishing up our last spoonfuls when a large, dark-haired woman asked for the microphone from Ian. She was dressed in jeans and a black fleece top. It was a common practice for people to address those gathered to offer information, prayers, or songs in support of protecting the water.

"I am Cheyenne," she began. "I hear there have been no sweats for women because there isn't anyone who is qualified to offer them."

I looked at Sarah with eyes raised and a hopeful expression on my face.

"Only women who have sundanced can offer sweats. And only women who have been passed the water can offer sweats. No others. I have sundanced, and I have been passed the water," she stated emphatically.

Sarah leaned in. "We may get to sweat."

Continuing, she dropped a random confession. "I want people to know I'm gay. I have spoken with my Elder about this, and he told me I am this way because I was abused as a child."

No, no, no, she just did not say that. I sat shocked and speechless and stared at her like I would a train wreck. *Fuck me.* I looked around, and most people had flat, benign expressions; no one was murmuring. I couldn't possibly be the only one who thought the queer community just got kicked in the short and curlies. *Fuck me again.*

"For the sweat, women are to wear skirts and have their shoulders covered. They should also bring tobacco. As soon as we know the time to go in, I'll post it here on the board."

The administration tent behind her had a whiteboard, mostly scrawled with people looking for people, needing rides or offering lifts.

"How can she say that?" I leaned in and whispered harshly to Sarah. "Does she realize what she said?"

"No, I don't think so. Are you going to sweat?"

"First I'm going to ask her if I have to wear a skirt."

I got the Cheyenne woman's attention when she came out of the administrative tent. "Hi, excuse me. Do Two-Spirited women have to wear skirts to sweat?"

She was curt. "I wear a skirt, and you're just like me." Then she walked away, accompanied by an older man. I was flustered by her dismissal and eagerness to get away from me. *You know you can't catch gay, especially if you're queer yourself.*

I wondered if the older man was her Elder. Was it possible that part of her work with him required a public confession, an airing of her sins in support of the heteronormative suppression of queer people? *Did I just say heteronormative? Yup.*

As I understood it, pre-contact cultures regarded multiple gender roles as complementary, not in opposition or even specifically binary, but as sacred gifts to the community. Those roles didn't rely on anatomy and were self-determined.

It was also said Two-Spirited people were given special status because of their ability to understand both the male and female perspectives. Gender-fluid members of the Nation were celebrated and valued as visionaries, healers, and medicine people.

In Indigenous languages, there are many and varied words used to describe those with diverse sexual and gender identities, but nothing as specific as Two-Spirit, which is an English word that surfaced in the '70s. It didn't matter until it mattered, compliments of the dominant culture.

I looked around, feeling lost. I was angry about her dismissal, but I was more saddened by her homophobia and unwillingness to accept herself, to be proud of who she was. I wanted to see her stand tall and be true to herself.

I sat heavily on the bench next to Sarah. "I'm not wearing a fucking skirt." I got annoyed because it was the first time I had sworn in camp. I looked around to see if anyone else had heard me. No one seemed to be paying attention.

A very large woman sat down heavily on the bench beside me. She was dressed in black sweatpants and a black t-shirt and was sweating profusely. Her name was Fish. It was really a nickname, a play on her last name, she told me. She leaned around me to say hello to Sarah. They had met earlier in the day. Fish was a freelance photographer from New York City and had landed in camp after getting a ride from Bismarck. She'd taken the train most of the way to North Dakota.

I pulled over a chair so we could sit in a small circle instead of trying to lean over and around each other. Fish, who was a lesbian, and I talked about our disappointment with the Cheyenne woman's manifesto-like confession, and about not feeling comfortable going to the sweat. She told us we weren't alone, that several women had complained, and there was going to be a women-only meeting with the Elders in a couple of hours at the Legal Aid tent on the way up Facebook Hill.

As much as I had invested in changing the narrative and wanting to have a voice, I kept thinking of Paula asking me to come home. Surrounded by people, I was feeling her absence even more keenly. *Is it because I wish she could be here with me, to appreciate my feeling of belonging, my sense of purpose, here at the end of the road? Or is it because, now that I know she wants me, I want to be there more than I want to be here?*

The larger question was: do I just want to be needed and loved no matter what, or do I want to be partnered because to be single again would be considered a failure? I realized I could get substantially lost in that question. Apparently, I have work to do, but there are miles ahead for contemplation and unpacking my baggage.

* * *

I squinted through the windshield and tried to make out the dark shapes further down the highway. I was on the only road heading north from camp. I was going home. *Are those lights? Is that a building or a washout or... a blockade? It is. Shit.*

I took my foot off the gas and slowed down when I saw a state trooper waving at me to stop. He had come out of his car, which was in the left lane, behind a Jersey wall concrete barrier. There was another barrier in the right lane. I stopped at the flag he indicated and waited. *Are they taking pictures? Are they radioing in my plates?*

After a few minutes, he signalled me to come ahead, and when I passed him, I couldn't see his eyes through the mirrored glasses under the large brim of his hat. There was no further acknowledgement when he directed me with a stiff palm around the barriers. Once through, I saw two National Guard soldiers dressed in camouflage and holding machine guns. They didn't smile either. I accelerated.

Earlier that morning, I woke up to a soggy and muddy camp. It had rained hard most of yesterday, continuing into the evening and overnight. After lunch and the drama of "sweatgate," I spent most of the afternoon and early evening tucked into my sleeping bag, reading a mystery novel.

Getting ready to leave, I managed to slip out of the Edge and into my boots and rain jacket while staying fairly dry. Ely's tent had sagged in a few places, taking on puddles of water. Nearby, several other tents were humbled, nearly broken, with slumping flies and tarps filled with water; some were completely flattened above humps of belongings, possibly people.

The real disaster, a petty one, was the dousing of the cooking fire overnight. No fire meant no coffee. When I got to the kitchen, several people were trying to light the fire from some meagre coals and wet kindling. The cheerier ones were optimistically dumping and filling percolators. The lack of coffee may have been the deciding factor in my choice to hit the road early.

While I was optimistically waiting for a latte, Sarah had come over and asked me to help her fix up Fish's tent. Fish had pitched it in a low area at the bottom of a hill, and all her belongings—clothes, sleeping bag, and pillow—were soaked from the rain. We dragged the tent onto a bit of a knoll, re-rigged it, and draped it with a tarp that Sarah had scavenged for additional protection.

I borrowed a hammer from a neighbouring camp and drove the tent and tarp ties into the ground as deeply as I could. "Should hold for ya, Fish."

It didn't take long to leave camp once I'd made my mind up. I said my goodbyes and hugged Fish, Sarah, Ian, and lots of other good people before going back to the Edge, where I had already tucked away and organized my stove and cooler. I joined a line of cars leaving camp. Some vehicles needed two or three runs at the muddy slope before reaching the gravel shoulder. Edge and I made it on the first run.

The map showed I'd be near the Missouri River soon, and I wondered if I'd get a glimpse of it from the road. I also wondered if Ely smiled his bashful smile when he found the three boiled eggs that I left at the door of his tent this morning. I was sad I wouldn't be able to give him a hug before I left, but I was hoping he'd see the eggs as my way of saying goodbye. I wished the best for him.

I knew that my leaving camp wasn't truly about the lack of hot coffee or even the rain and muddy conditions. Would I be that petty? No, it had everything to do with wanting to go home to Paula, and to myself in a convoluted way.

It was truly an honour to have shared space and spent time with good and true people, protecting the water and Mother Earth. I thought back to when I first heard the drums on the night I arrived in camp, understanding now that the road home would always be through Standing Rock.

ACKNOWLEDGEMENTS

Writing is a singular activity. For me, it's a process of circling the chair and, when seated, being inspired by friends and writers I admire.

While it may just be me in the seat, it takes a community to put out a book. I'm very grateful for the ongoing support and guidance of Inanna, specifically Publicist and Marketing Manager Renée Knapp, Editor Kaitlin Littlechild, Editor Ashley Rayner, and Board President Brenda Cranney.

To Val Fullard, thank you for a great cover and for your patience with my nudging of the torn section. I'd also like to thank Kimberley Griffith and Alicia Hibbert for their work in copy editing the final manuscript, as well as Judith Earnshaw for her careful proofreading.

A very special thank you needs to be said in spirit to Inanna Publications Editor-in-Chief Luciana Ricciutelli, who left us in December 2020. Luciana was a loving and genuine soul who always responded when I asked. From my heart to yours, maarsii, meegwetch, thank you.

As always, I'm very grateful for the feedback from the informal group of writers I belong to who were early readers of my stories. They are John Sifton, Robin Collins, Ken Bachman, and Colleen Pellatt. All wonderful writers and good people that make me feel safe and worthy.

Lastly, I need to thank my partner Paula for her love and unfailing confidence in me.

Credit: Paula Robert

Tradeswoman, artist, and teacher **Lorrie Potvin**, a queerishly Two-Spirited Métis, is the author of *Horses in the Sand: A Memoir* and *First Gear: A Motorcycle Memoir* (2015), published under the surname Jorgensen. She holds an Inter-Provincial Red Seal in Auto Body Repair and Refinishing and a diploma in Technological Education from Queen's University. Lorrie lives on a lake north of Kingston in the area served by the High Land Waters Métis Council. https://lorriepotvin.ca/

Also by Lorrie Potvin

First Gear: A Motorcycle Memoir